THE SYNERGY MINDSET: AI AND HUMAN FUTURE

MASTERING AI COLLABORATION FOR INNOVATION, ETHICS, AND A NEW RENAISSANCE

NATHALIE HARTE

First Edition 2025

Published by Haven of Words

CONTENTS

INTRODUCTION

As we reach the culmination of our exploration into the synergy between artificial intelligence and human potential, we stand on the brink of a transformative era. This book has illuminated the path towards a future where AI is not merely a tool, but a profound collaborator in our quest for innovation, ethical responsibility, and creative resurgence. By leveraging the HEART framework—Humanize, Evaluate, Adapt, Resonate, Transform—we have charted a course for nurturing a harmonious relationship with AI, one that is grounded in mutual respect and shared goals.

In envisioning this new Renaissance, we recognize the importance of human creativity and ethical foresight in steering the development and integration of AI technologies. The lessons drawn from historical parallels, such as the printing press and the Industrial Revolution, serve as reminders of our capacity to adapt and thrive amidst technological upheaval. These insights empower us to harness AI's potential while safeguarding our humanity.

The journey outlined in this book is not merely theoretical but calls for actionable steps. Leaders, technologists, and policymakers are urged to champion a mindset that sees AI as a partner. This collaboration promises to unlock unprecedented opportunities across diverse fields, from healthcare to finance, fostering a future where AI enhances rather than diminishes human experience.

As we look ahead, the responsibility rests with each of us to cultivate lifelong learning and resilience, embracing the rapid advancements in AI with a spirit of curiosity and ethics. By doing so, we lay the foundation for a future where AI and humans co-create a world defined by innovation, equity, and shared prosperity. Let this be the dawn of a new age, where the synergy of AI and human potential ushers in a brighter, more inclusive future for all.

Chapter 1: The AI Renaissance

Historical Parallels

Reflecting on our history, we see that each technological advancement has brought about a profound transformation in society, reshaping the very fabric of human life. The introduction of the printing press in the 15th century revolutionized the dissemination of knowledge, breaking the monopoly of the literate elite and democratizing information for the masses. This pivotal moment not only accelerated the spread of new ideas but also laid the groundwork for the Enlightenment and the scientific revolution. Similarly, the Industrial Revolution of the 18th and 19th centuries redefined industries and economies, shifting agrarian societies towards urbanization and mechanization. It was a time of both great upheaval and unprecedented growth, as human ingenuity met the power of machines, leading to increased productivity and the birth of modern industry.

Today, we stand at the cusp of another transformative era, driven by the rapid advancements in artificial intelligence. Just as the printing press and industrial machines once did,

AI holds the potential to redefine our world, impacting every sector from healthcare to finance, education to entertainment. Yet, with this potential comes a responsibility to navigate this new frontier thoughtfully and ethically. The lessons of the past teach us that while technology can be a powerful ally, it must be guided by human values and ethics to ensure it serves the greater good.

The synergy between AI and human potential is not just about leveraging technology for efficiency or productivity. It is about creating a partnership where AI complements human creativity, intuition, and empathy, rather than overshadowing them. This requires a shift in mindset, one that embraces AI as a collaborator in our journey towards progress. By looking to historical parallels, we can gain insights into how to approach this new relationship. Just as the printing press empowered individuals with knowledge, AI can empower us with tools to solve complex problems and innovate in ways previously unimaginable.

Moreover, the Industrial Revolution teaches us about the importance of adaptability and resilience in the face of change. As AI continues to evolve, we must cultivate a culture of lifelong learning and adaptability, preparing ourselves and future generations to thrive in an AI-enhanced world. This involves not only embracing technological skills but also fostering critical thinking, creativity, and emotional intelligence.

As we reflect on these historical parallels, it becomes clear that the future of AI and human collaboration is not predetermined. It is a narrative we are actively writing, shaped by the choices we make today. By learning from the past, we can chart a course that maximizes the benefits of AI while mitigating its risks, ensuring a future where technology and humanity coexist harmoniously. This is the challenge and the opportunity that lies before us, as we stand on the brink of the next great renaissance in human progress.

The HEART Framework

In the landscape of AI and human collaboration, a pivotal model emerges to guide this relationship: the HEART Framework. This framework serves as a beacon for navigating the complex interplay between human capabilities and artificial intelligence, promoting a partnership that is both ethical and innovative. At its core, the HEART Framework emphasizes five key principles:

Humanize, Evaluate, Adapt, Resonate, and Transform. These principles collectively foster an environment where AI is seen not as a replacement but as a complement to human ingenuity.

Humanizing AI involves imbuing artificial systems with empathy and understanding, ensuring that technology remains aligned with human values and societal norms. This principle advocates for the development of AI that respects and enhances human dignity, encouraging systems that are designed with a deep appreciation for the human experience. By prioritizing human-centric design, we ensure that AI technologies serve to augment human abilities rather than diminish them.

Evaluation within the HEART Framework refers to the continuous assessment of AI technologies to mitigate risks and seize opportunities. This involves a rigorous analysis of AI's impact across various sectors, from healthcare to finance, ensuring that its integration leads to beneficial outcomes. Effective evaluation requires a balanced approach that considers both the technical capabilities of AI and the ethical implications of its deployment.

Adaptation is crucial in a world where AI technologies evolve at an unprecedented pace. The HEART Framework encourages a mindset of lifelong learning and flexibility, empowering individuals and organizations to stay ahead of technological advancements. By fostering adaptability, we create a culture that is not only resilient to change but also proactive in leveraging new AI capabilities for innovative solutions.

Resonating with AI implies creating systems that align with human emotions and cultural contexts. This principle is about ensuring that AI technologies are not only functional but also culturally sensitive and emotionally intelligent. By developing AI that resonates with users on a personal level, we enhance user engagement and satisfaction, leading to more meaningful interactions between humans and machines.

Finally, the principle of Transformation within the HEART Framework envisions a future where AI catalyzes profound changes in society. This transformation is not merely about technological advancement but about redefining what it means to live and work in an AI-augmented world. By embracing transformative AI, we can unlock new possibilities for human achievement, driving progress that is inclusive and sustainable.

The HEART Framework thus offers a comprehensive approach to integrating AI into human society. It challenges us to rethink our relationship with technology, urging us to harness AI's potential while safeguarding human values. Through this framework, leaders, technologists, and policymakers are equipped to forge a future where AI and humanity thrive together, creating a synergy that propels us towards a new era of innovation and ethical progress.

Redefining Progress

Progress, as traditionally defined, has often been a linear pursuit of economic growth and technological advancement. Yet, in the context of the AI and human synergy, this understanding requires a profound transformation. Progress must be reimagined to encompass not only the technological and economic dimensions but also the social, ethical, and environmental aspects that contribute to holistic well-being. This redefinition calls for a shift from a purely output-driven mindset to one that values sustainability, equity, and human flourishing.

At the heart of this new paradigm is the recognition that AI, when harnessed thoughtfully, can be a catalyst for profound societal transformation. It challenges us to reconsider what it means to progress as a collective, urging us to integrate AI in ways that enhance human capabilities and address the pressing challenges of our time. By doing so, AI becomes a partner in crafting a future where progress is measured not just by GDP or technological milestones, but by the quality of life and the health of our planet.

This redefined progress requires a multi-faceted approach. It involves creating systems that prioritize ethical considerations and long-term impacts over short-term gains. It calls for policies that promote inclusivity and ensure that the benefits of AI advancements are distributed equitably across different segments of society. Furthermore, it demands an educational paradigm that prepares individuals to thrive in an AI-enhanced world, fostering skills that complement technological capabilities rather than compete with them.

The journey towards redefining progress is not without its challenges. It necessitates breaking free from entrenched ideologies and economic models that prioritize growth over sustainability. It requires a willingness to experiment with new frameworks and to embrace uncertainty as a space for innovation. Importantly, it involves engaging diverse voices in the conversation about the future we wish to build, ensuring that the vision of progress is inclusive and representative of our global community.

In redefining progress, we are also tasked with reevaluating the metrics by which we gauge success. Traditional indicators such as productivity and efficiency must be balanced with measures of social well-being, environmental health, and cultural richness. This holistic approach recognizes that true progress is achieved when technological advancements serve the broader goals of human and ecological flourishing.

As we stand at the intersection of AI and human potential, the opportunity to redefine progress is both a challenge and a privilege. It invites us to envision a future where technology amplifies our best qualities and addresses our most significant challenges. By redefining progress, we embrace a vision of a world where AI and humanity co-create paths to a more equitable, sustainable, and vibrant future. This is the essence of the synergy mindset—an approach that sees AI not as a replacement for human endeavor, but as a powerful ally in the quest for a truly progressive society.

AI as an Ally

In the ever-evolving landscape of technology, artificial intelligence stands as a beacon of possibility, offering transformative potential across all facets of human endeavor. The relationship between AI and humanity is not one of adversarial tension but of collaborative synergy, where each complements and elevates the other. This partnership heralds a new era of innovation, where AI acts as a catalyst for human creativity and problem-solving.

The HEART framework encapsulates this philosophy, guiding the integration of AI into our lives in a manner that is ethical, responsible, and forward-thinking. By humanizing AI, we acknowledge its role not as a replacement for human intelligence but as an extension of it. This perspective encourages the development of AI systems that prioritize empathy and understanding, fostering a coexistence that values human input and creativity.

Evaluation is a critical component of this framework, necessitating a thorough assessment of AI's capabilities and limitations. This involves scrutinizing the ethical implications of AI deployment across various industries, from healthcare to finance, ensuring that its application does not compromise human values or rights. By maintaining a vigilant approach to AI integration, we can mitigate risks while harnessing opportunities for growth and innovation.

Adaptation is imperative in a world where AI technology advances at an unprecedented pace. Embracing a mindset of lifelong learning allows individuals and organizations to remain agile, continuously updating their skills and knowledge to keep pace with technological advancements. This adaptability ensures that AI remains a tool for empowerment rather than a source of obsolescence.

Resonance within the HEART framework speaks to the harmonious integration of AI into the human experience. By aligning AI applications with human needs and aspirations, we create systems that enhance our capabilities rather than detract from them. This alignment encourages a future where AI-driven solutions resonate with societal goals, driving progress in a manner that is both sustainable and equitable.

Transformation, the final pillar of the HEART framework, is where the true potential of AI as an ally is realized. Through transformative AI-human partnerships, we can tackle complex global challenges, from climate change to healthcare inequities, with renewed vigor and perspective. These collaborations have the power to unlock unprecedented levels of innovation, spurring a new renaissance of human achievement.

AI's role as an ally is not merely a futuristic vision but a present reality, one that requires deliberate and thoughtful action to realize its full potential. By embracing AI as a partner, we open the door to a future where technology and humanity coexist in harmony, each enhancing the other's strengths. This synergy is the cornerstone of a brighter, more innovative future, where AI serves not as a threat but as a trusted ally in the ongoing journey of human progress.

Chapter 2: Human Potential Unleashed

Creativity and AI

In the intricate dance between human creativity and artificial intelligence, we uncover a landscape rich with potential and possibility. As AI continues to evolve, it challenges and expands the boundaries of human creativity, acting not merely as a tool but as a collaborator in the creative process. This relationship prompts us to reconsider what it means to be creative and how AI can enhance this quintessentially human trait.

Creativity has historically been seen as a uniquely human endeavor, characterized by the ability to imagine, invent, and innovate. It is an expression of individuality and a reflection of our deepest thoughts and emotions. However, with the advent of AI, we are witnessing a transformation in how creativity is understood and expressed. AI systems, equipped with vast computational power and access to extensive datasets, can generate art, music, and literature, often indistinguishable from that created by humans.

This shift invites a reevaluation of the creative process. AI can analyze patterns, predict trends, and offer insights that might elude even the most perceptive human minds. For instance, in the realm of visual arts, AI can generate original artworks by learning from a plethora of styles and techniques. In music, AI can compose symphonies that echo the complexity and emotion of human compositions. These capabilities do not diminish human creativity but rather augment it, offering new tools and perspectives that can inspire novel forms of expression.

Yet, the integration of AI into the creative process raises important questions about authorship and originality. When an AI system creates, who is the true author—the machine or the human who programmed it? This question challenges our traditional notions of creativity and intellectual property, prompting a need for new frameworks that recognize the collaborative nature of human-AI creativity.

Moreover, AI's role in creativity extends beyond the arts. In fields such as science and engineering, AI assists in designing experiments, optimizing solutions, and uncovering new knowledge. It can simulate complex systems and predict outcomes with remarkable accuracy, enabling human creators to push the boundaries of what is possible. This synergy between AI and human creativity has the potential to drive innovation across all sectors, leading to breakthroughs that can address some of the world's most pressing challenges.

However, to harness the full potential of AI in creative endeavors, we must cultivate a mindset that views AI as a partner rather than a competitor. This requires fostering an environment where experimentation and collaboration are encouraged, and where the unique strengths of both humans and machines are leveraged. By embracing this collaborative approach, we can unlock new dimensions of creativity and innovation, paving the way for a future where human and artificial intelligence coexist harmoniously.

In this new era, the synergy between AI and human creativity is not just a possibility; it is an imperative. As we continue to explore this dynamic relationship, we are reminded that creativity is not a static trait but a living, evolving process. With AI as our ally, we stand on the brink of a creative renaissance, one that holds the promise of transforming our world in ways we have yet to imagine.

Innovation Synergies

In the evolving landscape where artificial intelligence and human innovation intersect, the potential for creating synergies that propel us into a new era of advancement is immense. This subchapter delves into these synergies, exploring how the collaboration between AI and human creativity can unlock unprecedented opportunities for growth and transformation. By examining this dynamic partnership, we uncover the layers of potential that lie within the fusion of human ingenuity and machine intelligence.

One of the core aspects of this synergy is the ability to leverage AI as a tool that enhances human capabilities rather than replacing them. AI can process and analyze vast amounts of data at speeds beyond human reach, providing insights that were previously unattainable. When these insights are coupled with human intuition and creativity, they lead to innovative solutions that address complex challenges across various sectors. This cooperative interaction not only amplifies the potential for problem-solving but also fosters an environment where creativity is continuously nurtured.

Moreover, the integration of AI into human-driven processes encourages a reevaluation of traditional

20

methodologies. It prompts industries to rethink their strategies and operations, leading to more efficient and effective outcomes. For instance, in healthcare, AI can assist in diagnosing diseases with greater accuracy and speed, allowing medical professionals to focus on patient care and personalized treatment plans. This collaborative approach not only improves service delivery but also enhances the quality of care, showcasing the transformative power of AI when synergized with human expertise.

Another dimension of innovation synergies is the democratization of technology and knowledge. AI-driven platforms can provide access to information and educational resources to a broader audience, breaking down barriers that have historically limited learning and growth opportunities. This democratization fosters an inclusive environment where diverse voices contribute to the innovation process, enriching the collective pool of ideas and solutions. By empowering individuals with the tools and knowledge to engage with AI, we pave the way for a more equitable and innovative future.

Furthermore, the synergy between AI and human creativity is not limited to enhancing existing processes but also extends to the creation of entirely new paradigms. As AI continues to evolve, it inspires novel forms of art, design, and expression, pushing the boundaries of what is possible. This creative partnership challenges conventional norms and encourages experimentation, leading to breakthroughs that redefine industries and experiences. By embracing this collaborative potential, we unlock new avenues for artistic and technological exploration.

In this context, it is crucial to foster an environment that supports continuous learning and adaptation. As AI technologies advance, the skills required to harness their potential also evolve. Encouraging a mindset of lifelong learning ensures that individuals and organizations remain agile and responsive to the changing landscape. This adaptability is key to maximizing the benefits of AI-human synergies, enabling us to navigate the complexities of the future with confidence and creativity.

Ultimately, the synergy between AI and human innovation represents a powerful alliance that holds the promise of driving significant progress. By embracing this partnership, we can unlock new potentials, create transformative solutions, and shape a future where technology and humanity coexist in harmony, each enhancing the other's capabilities.

Humanize AI

In the evolving landscape of artificial intelligence, the concept of humanizing AI stands as a beacon of our shared future. This involves crafting an AI ecosystem that resonates with human values, ethics, and creativity, fostering a partnership rather than a hierarchical relationship. The essence of humanizing AI lies in integrating empathy and understanding into its algorithms, ensuring that AI can not only perform tasks but also appreciate the nuances of human emotions and contexts.

The journey to humanize AI begins with acknowledging the multifaceted nature of intelligence. Human intelligence is not merely computational; it is emotional, ethical, and creative. To truly humanize AI, we must infuse these elements into its core. This requires a shift from viewing AI as a mere tool to recognizing it as a collaborator in our creative and problem-solving processes.

Incorporating empathy into AI systems is a pivotal step. This involves designing AI that can understand and respond to human emotions in a meaningful way. By doing so, AI can enhance its interactions with humans, making them more natural and intuitive. This is particularly crucial in fields such as healthcare, where empathetic AI can support medical professionals in providing compassionate care.

Ethical considerations are also paramount in the humanization process. As AI systems gain more autonomy, ensuring they adhere to ethical guidelines becomes critical. This involves embedding ethical decision-making frameworks within AI, enabling them to make choices that align with human morals and societal norms. It is about creating AI that not only understands the difference between right and wrong but also acts in ways that promote human welfare and dignity.

Creativity is another dimension where AI can be humanized. By leveraging AI's analytical capabilities alongside human creativity, we can unlock new possibilities in art, design, and innovation. AI can serve as a muse, offering unique insights and perspectives that inspire human creators to push the boundaries of their work.

The synergy between AI and humans can lead to a future where technology amplifies human potential rather than diminishing it. By focusing on humanizing AI, we ensure that this powerful technology serves as a catalyst for personal and societal growth. This requires ongoing collaboration between technologists, ethicists, and creatives to continually refine AI systems, making them more aligned with human-centric values.

Ultimately, the goal is to cultivate an AI ecosystem that mirrors the diversity and depth of human intelligence. This means developing AI that is not only capable of performing complex tasks but also enriching the human experience. By humanizing AI, we are not just enhancing its utility but also ensuring that it contributes positively to the tapestry of human life.

In this harmonious convergence of AI and humanity, we find the potential for a new renaissance—one where technology and human values are inextricably linked, driving progress and innovation in tandem. By embracing this vision, we pave the way for a future where AI is not just smart but also wise, capable of understanding and enhancing the human condition.

Bridging Gaps

In the evolving landscape of AI and human interaction, the notion of bridging gaps serves as a pivotal theme. The synergy between artificial intelligence and human intuition isn't merely about coexistence but about fostering a cooperative relationship that enhances both entities' capabilities. This chapter delves into how bridging these gaps can transform challenges into opportunities, creating a future where AI complements human ingenuity.

The first step in bridging these gaps is recognizing the inherent strengths and limitations of both humans and AI. Humans possess emotional intelligence, creativity, and ethical reasoning, which are essential for navigating complex moral landscapes and fostering innovation. On the other hand, AI excels in processing vast amounts of data, identifying patterns, and performing repetitive tasks with precision. By acknowledging these differences, we can begin to construct a framework where each can enhance the other's strengths.

Collaboration between AI and humans should be seen as a partnership where mutual growth is the goal. For instance, in healthcare, AI can assist in diagnosing diseases by analyzing medical images with greater speed and accuracy than a human could. However, the human touch remains indispensable in patient care, offering empathy and understanding that machines cannot replicate. This partnership not only improves efficiency but also elevates the quality of service by combining the best of both worlds.

Moreover, bridging gaps involves addressing the ethical considerations that arise with AI's integration into society. As AI systems become more autonomous, ensuring they align with human values and ethical standards becomes crucial. This requires a commitment to transparency and accountability in AI development and deployment. Policymakers, technologists, and ethicists must collaborate to create guidelines that safeguard against misuse while promoting innovation.

Education and continuous learning play a critical role in this bridging process. As AI technologies evolve, so too must our skills and knowledge. Lifelong learning initiatives that focus on digital literacy and AI competencies can empower individuals to thrive in an AI-augmented world. Educational systems must adapt to foster critical thinking and adaptability, preparing future generations to work alongside AI effectively.

Finally, fostering a culture of inclusivity and diversity in AI development is essential for bridging gaps. Diverse teams bring varied perspectives, leading to more innovative solutions and fairer AI systems. By ensuring that voices from different backgrounds are heard and considered, we can develop AI technologies that are more representative of and beneficial to all segments of society.

In essence, bridging gaps between AI and humans is about creating a harmonious relationship where both can flourish. It requires a thoughtful approach that considers ethical implications, promotes continuous learning, and embraces diversity. By doing so, we unlock the full potential of AI as a transformative partner in our journey towards a more innovative and equitable future.

Chapter 3: Building AI Resilience

Adaptability and Growth

In the ever-evolving landscape of technology, adaptability emerges as an essential human trait, enabling individuals and societies to navigate the rapid changes brought about by artificial intelligence. This growth mindset, characterized by openness to new experiences and a willingness to learn, is crucial as AI continues to reshape various facets of life. Human adaptability is not merely about survival but thriving in a world where AI becomes an integral partner. It involves the continuous development of skills and knowledge, fostering resilience in the face of technological advancements.

The synergy between AI and human potential is most evident in the transformative power of adaptability. As AI systems become more sophisticated, they demand a parallel evolution in human capabilities. This dynamic relationship invites a rethinking of traditional roles and the creation of new opportunities for collaboration. People who embrace a mindset of growth are better positioned to leverage AI, using it as a tool to enhance creativity, improve decision-making, and solve complex problems.

The HEART framework within this context provides a pathway for cultivating adaptability. By humanizing interactions with AI, individuals can build trust and understanding, paving the way for more meaningful collaborations. Evaluating AI's impact on personal and professional growth encourages a proactive approach to change, enabling individuals to anticipate challenges and seize opportunities. Adapting to the fast-paced nature of AI development requires a commitment to lifelong learning, where education and skills acquisition are continuous processes.

This adaptability is not just an individual endeavor but a collective one. Organizations and communities must foster environments that encourage experimentation and innovation. This involves creating spaces where failure is seen as a learning opportunity and success is measured by the ability to adapt and grow. By resonating with these principles, people can transform their relationship with technology, viewing AI not as a competitor but as an ally that amplifies human potential.

In this journey of adaptability and growth, historical contexts provide valuable lessons. The Industrial Revolution, for instance, demanded a significant shift in skills and societal structures, much like the current AI revolution. Those who adapted thrived, while others who resisted change faced obsolescence. Today, the stakes are higher, with AI impacting every sector from healthcare to finance, necessitating a more agile and innovative approach.

Ultimately, the adaptability and growth mindset is about embracing change with a sense of curiosity and optimism. It is about understanding that the future is not predetermined but shaped by the collective actions of individuals who dare to dream and innovate. By nurturing these qualities, humanity can harness the full potential of AI, ensuring that it serves as a force for good, driving progress while preserving the core values that define our human experience.

Lifelong Learning

In the evolving landscape of the 21st century, the concept of lifelong learning emerges as a critical pillar in the synergy between artificial intelligence and human potential. This dynamic relationship is not merely about acquiring new skills but about fostering a mindset that embraces continuous growth and adaptation. As AI technologies advance at an unprecedented pace, the necessity for individuals to remain agile and open to learning becomes increasingly paramount. This ongoing educational journey is not confined to traditional academic settings but extends into everyday interactions with technology.

Lifelong learning, in this context, is an empowering approach that equips individuals with the tools to navigate the complexities of a tech-driven world. It encourages a proactive stance towards knowledge acquisition, where curiosity is the driving force. This mindset is essential for harnessing AI's capabilities effectively, ensuring that individuals can leverage these tools to enhance their personal and professional lives.

The HEART framework, introduced in this book, serves as a beacon guiding this lifelong learning journey. By Humanizing AI, individuals are encouraged to see technology not as a replacement but as an extension of human capability. This perspective fosters an environment where learning is a collaborative process between man and machine. Evaluating and adapting to new information becomes second nature, allowing for a seamless integration of AI into daily life. This adaptability is crucial as industries from healthcare to finance undergo rapid transformations driven by AI.

Moreover, lifelong learning in the age of AI is about more than just keeping up with technological advancements. It's about cultivating a deeper understanding of the ethical implications and responsibilities that come with these tools. As AI systems become more integrated into decision-making processes, individuals must develop the ability to critically assess these systems, ensuring they align with human values and ethics.

The book emphasizes the importance of creating meaningful AI-human partnerships that resonate with transformative potential. This involves not only adapting to new technologies but also contributing to their evolution. By engaging with AI as active participants rather than passive consumers, individuals can influence the trajectory of these technologies, ensuring they serve the broader goals of society.

In this new paradigm, lifelong learning becomes a collective endeavor, where communities and organizations support and nurture this mindset. Collaborative platforms and networks play a vital role in disseminating knowledge and fostering innovation. This shared learning experience breaks down barriers, creating a more inclusive environment where diverse perspectives contribute to the development of AI.

Ultimately, the pursuit of lifelong learning in the context of AI is about preparing for a future where technology and humanity coexist harmoniously. It is about building resilience and adaptability, ensuring that individuals are not only prepared for the challenges of tomorrow but are also capable of shaping a future that reflects their aspirations and values. By committing to this path of continuous learning, society can unlock the full potential of AI, transforming challenges into opportunities for growth and innovation.

Resilient Systems

In the ever-evolving landscape of technology, the concept of resilience emerges as a cornerstone for building sustainable systems that can withstand and adapt to the myriad challenges of the modern world. Resilience in systems is not merely about withstanding shocks but thriving amid them. As we delve into the realm of resilient systems, we recognize the intricate dance between robustness and adaptability, where each component is designed to not only survive but evolve in response to external pressures.

In our pursuit of resilient systems, we must first understand the dynamic nature of change itself. Systems today are more interconnected than ever, and this interdependence, while offering unprecedented opportunities for growth and innovation, also introduces complex vulnerabilities. A resilient system anticipates these vulnerabilities, incorporating flexibility and redundancy as foundational principles. Flexibility allows for swift adaptation to unexpected changes, while redundancy ensures that failure in one part does not lead to a collapse of the whole.

The synergy between artificial intelligence and human ingenuity plays a pivotal role in crafting these resilient systems. AI, with its capacity for rapid data processing and pattern recognition, can foresee potential disruptions and provide real-time solutions, thereby enhancing the system's ability to adapt. Human oversight, on the other hand, ensures that these solutions are aligned with ethical considerations and long-term objectives, creating a balanced approach to resilience.

Moreover, the concept of resilience extends beyond the technical framework to encompass cultural and organizational dimensions. Organizations must cultivate a culture of resilience, where learning from failures is encouraged, and innovation is driven by curiosity rather than fear. This cultural resilience is what empowers teams to pivot and adapt, ensuring that the organization remains agile and responsive to change.

In practice, building resilient systems involves a continuous process of assessment and iteration. It requires a proactive stance on risk management, where potential threats are identified and mitigated before they manifest. This proactive approach is complemented by a feedback loop that allows systems to learn from past experiences, refining their strategies and operations over time.

To illustrate, consider the application of resilient systems in critical infrastructure, such as healthcare or finance. In these sectors, the ability to maintain functionality during crises is paramount. By integrating AI-driven predictive analytics, these systems can anticipate demand surges or potential failures, enabling them to allocate resources efficiently and maintain service continuity. Similarly, the use of blockchain technology in financial systems can enhance transparency and security, further bolstering resilience.

Ultimately, the pursuit of resilient systems is a journey of continuous improvement, where the interplay of technology and human insight creates a robust framework capable of navigating the complexities of the modern world. As we advance, the lessons learned from building resilient systems will not only safeguard our technological infrastructure but also inspire a broader application of resilience in all facets of life, fostering a future where adaptability and sustainability are at the forefront of progress.

Technology Integration

In an era where technology permeates every facet of life, the integration of AI into the human experience is not merely a technical endeavor but a profound transformation of our societal fabric. As we stand at this crossroads, the essence of technology integration lies in harmonizing the capabilities of AI with human potential, fostering a relationship that enhances rather than diminishes our intrinsic abilities. The HEART Framework serves as a guiding principle in this journey, emphasizing the need to

Humanize, Evaluate, Adapt, Resonate, and Transform our interactions with AI.

Humanizing technology begins with recognizing AI as an extension of human ingenuity. It involves embedding empathy and ethical considerations into AI systems, ensuring that technology reflects our core values and enhances our collective well-being. By doing so, we create AI that not only performs tasks but also understands and aligns with human emotions and societal norms, leading to more meaningful and impactful collaborations.

Evaluation of AI's role in our lives necessitates a critical examination of its potential and pitfalls. It requires a balanced approach where the benefits of AI, such as increased efficiency and innovation, are weighed against the risks, including privacy concerns and ethical dilemmas. This evaluation process is crucial in setting boundaries and guidelines that protect human interests while allowing AI to flourish within defined parameters.

Adaptation in the context of technology integration involves cultivating a mindset of continuous learning and flexibility. As AI evolves, so must our skills and approaches. Embracing lifelong learning ensures that individuals and organizations remain relevant and competitive in a rapidly changing landscape. This adaptability is key to harnessing AI's full potential and driving progress across various sectors, from healthcare to education.

Resonating with AI implies creating systems that echo human creativity and cultural diversity. It is about designing AI that complements human creativity, enabling new forms of expression and innovation. By resonating with human aspirations and cultural narratives, AI becomes a tool for empowerment, allowing diverse voices to be heard and fostering a more inclusive global community.

Finally, the transformative power of AI lies in its ability to redefine what is possible. Through strategic integration, AI can unlock new opportunities for growth and development, transforming industries and creating novel solutions to complex challenges. This transformation, however, must be guided by a vision that prioritizes human dignity and societal progress, ensuring that technology serves as a catalyst for a better future.

In this dynamic interplay between AI and human potential, the focus should remain on creating symbiotic relationships that enhance human capabilities. By integrating technology thoughtfully and responsibly, we pave the way for a future where AI and humanity coexist harmoniously, driving innovation and progress while preserving the essence of what it means to be human.

Chapter 4: Innovation through Collaboration

Cross-Industry Insights

The interplay of artificial intelligence across various industries unveils a tapestry of transformation that reshapes the very fabric of how we conduct business and innovate. Within this landscape, AI emerges not merely as a tool but as a collaborative partner, reimagining efficiency and creativity. In healthcare, AI-driven diagnostics and predictive analytics offer new avenues for early detection and personalized treatment, enhancing patient outcomes while alleviating the burdens on healthcare professionals. By analyzing vast datasets, AI identifies patterns and correlations that elude human perception, thus empowering practitioners with insights that were once beyond reach.

In the financial sector, AI algorithms are revolutionizing risk management and fraud detection. By continuously learning from transactional data, these systems adapt to evolving threats, offering security and precision in an ever-changing digital economy. This evolution is not without challenges, as the integration of AI demands a reevaluation of trust and ethical considerations. Nonetheless, the synergy between human oversight and machine learning fosters a resilient financial ecosystem that balances innovation with accountability.

Manufacturing stands on the brink of a new industrial revolution, driven by AI's capacity to optimize production lines and supply chains. Through predictive maintenance and real-time data analysis, AI enhances operational efficiency, reducing downtime and resource wastage. This transformation extends to the workforce, where AI augments human capabilities, fostering a collaborative environment that values both human ingenuity and machine precision.

The creative industries, once thought to be the exclusive domain of human imagination, are now enriched by AI's generative capabilities. From music composition to visual arts, AI acts as a muse and collaborator, expanding the boundaries of artistic expression. This partnership challenges traditional notions of authorship and creativity, prompting a reimagining of what it means to be an artist in the digital age.

Education, too, is undergoing a metamorphosis, as AI personalizes learning experiences and democratizes access to knowledge. Adaptive learning platforms cater to individual needs, empowering learners to progress at their own pace and style. This customization not only enhances educational outcomes but also prepares a future workforce adept at navigating the complexities of an AI-integrated world.

Across these sectors, a common thread emerges: the necessity for a mindset shift that embraces AI as a catalyst for progress rather than a threat to human employment and creativity. This requires leaders and policymakers to cultivate an environment where AI's potential is harnessed responsibly, ensuring that technological advancements do not eclipse ethical considerations. By fostering a culture of continuous learning and adaptation, industries can navigate the AI revolution with confidence, unlocking unprecedented opportunities for growth and innovation.

Reflecting on these insights, it becomes apparent that the future is not a binary choice between humanity and technology, but rather a harmonious coexistence where each amplifies the other's strengths. As we stand at the crossroads of possibility, the path forward is illuminated by the collaborative spirit that defines the synergy mindset.

Collaborative Mindset

The essence of a collaborative mindset lies in the ability to perceive AI not as a competing force, but as an integral partner in the tapestry of human progress. By fostering a mindset that is open to collaboration, individuals and organizations can unlock new potentials that neither AI nor humans could achieve alone. This symbiotic relationship is rooted in mutual respect and understanding, where both parties bring unique strengths to the table. Humans, with their innate creativity, emotional intelligence, and ethical reasoning, complement AI's capacity for data processing, pattern recognition, and relentless efficiency.

To cultivate this mindset, it is crucial to begin with a foundation of trust and transparency. Organizations must prioritize clear communication about the capabilities and limitations of AI systems. This involves educating team members on AI's role within the organization and creating an environment where questions and concerns can be openly addressed. Trust is further solidified by ensuring that AI systems are aligned with human values and ethical standards, reinforcing the idea that AI serves to enhance, not replace, human efforts.

Another cornerstone of the collaborative mindset is adaptability. As AI technologies evolve, so too must the strategies and frameworks that govern their use. This requires a commitment to lifelong learning and a willingness to embrace change. By staying informed about the latest advancements in AI, individuals and organizations can remain agile and responsive to new opportunities and challenges. This adaptability also extends to the workplace, where flexible structures and roles allow for seamless integration of AI into existing processes.

The collaborative mindset also emphasizes the importance of diversity and inclusion. By bringing together a wide range of perspectives, organizations can ensure that AI systems are designed to be equitable and accessible to all. This diversity of thought not only leads to more innovative solutions but also helps to mitigate biases that can arise in AI algorithms. By actively seeking out and valuing different viewpoints, organizations can create AI systems that truly reflect the diverse needs of their users.

Finally, a collaborative mindset requires a focus on shared goals and outcomes. By aligning AI efforts with the broader mission and vision of the organization, teams can work together towards common objectives. This alignment fosters a sense of purpose and unity, motivating individuals to contribute their best efforts toward achieving these goals. It also encourages collaboration across different departments and disciplines, breaking down silos and fostering a culture of innovation.

In sum, developing a collaborative mindset is essential for harnessing the full potential of AI-human partnerships. By building trust, embracing adaptability, valuing diversity, and aligning on shared goals, individuals and organizations can create a future where AI and humans thrive together, driving progress and innovation in unprecedented ways.

Resonate with AI

In a world where artificial intelligence steadily permeates every aspect of our lives, finding harmony between human intuition and AI's analytical prowess becomes paramount. The chapter delves into the essence of resonance, a concept crucial for fostering a profound connection between human values and AI capabilities. This resonance is not merely about aligning technical functions with human needs; it is about creating a deeper, more meaningful relationship where AI acts as an extension of human will and creativity.

AI, with its vast computational abilities, offers unprecedented opportunities to enhance decision-making, creativity, and problem-solving. However, to truly resonate with AI, we must first understand and acknowledge the unique strengths it brings to the table. AI's ability to process and analyze vast quantities of data at lightning speed complements the human capacity for empathy, ethical reasoning, and innovative thinking. By leveraging these complementary strengths, we can create systems that are not only efficient but also aligned with human values and societal goals.

The journey towards resonance with AI requires a shift in perspective, one that embraces AI as a partner in the creative process rather than a mere tool. This partnership is founded on mutual respect, where AI systems are designed with a deep understanding of human contexts and needs. Such systems are not only reactive but also proactive, anticipating human needs and adapting accordingly. This requires a collaborative design process involving diverse stakeholders, including technologists, ethicists, and users, to ensure that AI systems are inclusive and equitable.

Moreover, resonating with AI involves a commitment to lifelong learning and adaptation. As AI technologies evolve, so must our understanding and skills. This dynamic interplay between human and machine learning fosters a culture of continuous improvement and innovation. By staying informed and adaptable, individuals and organizations can harness the full potential of AI, driving progress in ways that are both responsible and sustainable.

The chapter also highlights the importance of transparency and accountability in AI systems. To build trust and ensure that AI resonates with human values, it is essential to develop systems that are understandable and interpretable. Users should have clarity on how AI systems make decisions and the underlying data and algorithms that drive those decisions. This transparency fosters trust and empowers users to make informed decisions about how they interact with AI.

Ultimately, resonating with AI is about creating a symbiotic relationship where human creativity and ethical reasoning are amplified by AI's computational power. This synergy can lead to innovations that not only solve complex problems but also enhance the human experience in meaningful ways. By embracing this holistic approach, we can pave the way for a future where AI and humanity thrive together, each enhancing the other's capabilities and potential.

Transformative Partnerships

In the evolving landscape of the 21st century, the collaboration between artificial intelligence and human intellect is not merely a possibility but an imperative. This alliance is reshaping industries, redefining roles, and revamping processes in ways that were once unimaginable. At the heart of this transformation lies the potential for partnerships that transcend traditional boundaries, fostering a synergy that leverages the strengths of both entities. The essence of transformative partnerships is rooted in mutual respect and understanding, where AI is not seen as a mere tool, but as a collaborator capable of augmenting human capabilities.

The foundational premise of such partnerships is the recognition of AI's ability to process vast amounts of data and identify patterns beyond human capacity. When combined with human intuition, creativity, and ethical considerations, these partnerships can drive innovation and efficiency to new heights. For instance, in healthcare, AI can analyze medical records at an unprecedented speed, providing doctors with insights that enhance diagnostic accuracy and personalize treatment plans. Similarly, in finance, AI algorithms can predict market trends with remarkable precision, enabling financial experts to make informed decisions that optimize investment strategies.

However, the success of these partnerships hinges on the establishment of a framework that emphasizes ethical considerations and responsible implementation. The HEART framework—Humanize, Evaluate, Adapt, Resonate, Transform—serves as a guiding principle for fostering these collaborations. By humanizing AI, we ensure that technology serves to enhance human experiences rather than replace them. Evaluation of AI's impact across various sectors allows for the identification of opportunities and risks, ensuring that its integration is beneficial and sustainable.

Adaptability is crucial in a rapidly changing technological environment. As AI continues to evolve, so must our approaches to integrating it into our daily lives and industries. Lifelong learning and continuous adaptation are necessary to remain relevant and effective in utilizing AI's capabilities. Moreover, the resonance of AI-human partnerships must be felt across all levels of society, promoting inclusivity and accessibility to ensure that the benefits of AI are shared equitably.

Ultimately, the transformative potential of AI-human partnerships lies in their ability to drive progress without compromising human values. By positioning AI as an ally, we pave the way for a future where technology and humanity coexist harmoniously, each enhancing the other. This vision of collaboration not only propels us into an era of unprecedented innovation but also ensures that the human element remains at the forefront of technological advancement. In this way, transformative partnerships become a catalyst for a new renaissance, one where progress is measured not just by technological achievements, but by the enrichment of human lives.

Chapter 5: Ethical Navigation

Responsible AI Use

In the rapidly evolving landscape of artificial intelligence, the need for responsible use has become paramount. As we stand on the brink of a new era, the integration of AI into our societies presents both unprecedented opportunities and profound challenges. The key to navigating this complex terrain lies in fostering a mindset that views AI not as an adversary, but as a partner in innovation and progress.

This partnership begins with a deep understanding of the ethical implications of AI deployment. It's essential to recognize that AI systems, while powerful, are not infallible. They reflect the biases and assumptions embedded in their algorithms by human designers. Thus, ensuring that these systems operate fairly and equitably requires ongoing vigilance. This involves not only technical adjustments but also a commitment to transparency and accountability.

Moreover, responsible AI use demands a proactive approach to privacy and data protection. As AI systems become increasingly integral to our daily lives, they gather vast amounts of personal data. Safeguarding this information is crucial to maintaining public trust and preventing misuse. Organizations must implement robust data governance frameworks that prioritize user consent and data minimization.

Another critical aspect of responsible AI use is the need for inclusivity in AI development. This means actively involving diverse voices in the design and deployment of AI technologies. By ensuring that a wide range of perspectives are considered, we can create AI systems that are more representative of, and responsive to, the needs of all individuals.

Furthermore, the responsible use of AI extends to its impact on the workforce. Automation and AI-driven processes are reshaping industries at an unprecedented pace. While this transformation offers efficiency gains, it also poses the risk of job displacement. To mitigate these effects, it is crucial to invest in upskilling and reskilling initiatives. By equipping workers with the skills needed to thrive in an AI-enhanced economy, we can facilitate a smoother transition and ensure that the benefits of AI are widely shared.

At the heart of responsible AI use is the principle of collaboration. The synergy between human creativity and machine intelligence can unlock new possibilities for innovation. However, this requires a deliberate effort to foster collaboration across disciplines and sectors. By cultivating a culture of openness and shared learning, we can harness the full potential of AI as a tool for societal good.

Ultimately, the responsible use of AI is a shared responsibility. It calls for concerted action from governments, businesses, and individuals alike. Policymakers must establish clear regulatory frameworks that guide AI development and use, while businesses should lead by example in adopting ethical AI practices. Meanwhile, individuals can contribute by staying informed and advocating for AI systems that align with our shared values.

In embracing these principles, we can chart a course towards a future where AI serves as a catalyst for human flourishing. By prioritizing ethical considerations and fostering inclusive innovation, we can ensure that AI enriches our societies and enhances our collective well-being.

Ethical Dilemmas

In the rapidly evolving landscape of artificial intelligence, the intersection of technology and humanity presents profound ethical dilemmas. As AI systems become increasingly integrated into our personal and professional lives, we face challenges that require us to reconsider fundamental questions about autonomy, privacy, and the essence of being human. These dilemmas are not merely theoretical but have tangible implications on how we govern, interact, and innovate.

One of the most pressing ethical concerns is the balance between innovation and privacy. AI's capacity to analyze vast amounts of data offers unprecedented opportunities for advancements in fields like healthcare and finance. However, this potential comes with the risk of infringing on individual privacy. The ability of AI to track personal habits, predict behaviors, and even influence decisions raises questions about consent and surveillance. As custodians of this technology, we must navigate these waters with a commitment to safeguarding individual rights while fostering innovation.

Another critical dilemma lies in the realm of decision-making. AI systems, designed to assist or even replace human judgment in various sectors, challenge the concept of accountability. When an AI system makes a decision, who is responsible for the outcome? This question becomes particularly poignant in sectors such as healthcare, where AI-driven diagnostics and treatment plans can significantly impact lives. Establishing clear lines of accountability and ensuring that AI systems are transparent and understandable are essential steps in addressing this ethical conundrum.

Furthermore, the potential for AI to perpetuate and even amplify societal biases presents another ethical challenge. AI systems learn from existing data, which often reflects historical biases and inequalities. If unchecked, AI can reinforce these biases, leading to discriminatory outcomes in areas like hiring, law enforcement, and lending. This necessitates a proactive approach to AI development, one that prioritizes fairness and inclusivity from the outset.

The concept of autonomy also comes to the fore in discussions about AI ethics. As AI systems become more autonomous, the potential for them to act independently of human oversight increases. This raises questions about the extent to which we should allow machines to operate without human intervention and the potential consequences of such autonomy. The challenge lies in designing AI that can operate effectively while remaining under human control and aligned with human values.

In grappling with these dilemmas, we must also consider the broader implications of AI on the human experience. AI has the potential to redefine what it means to work, learn, and create. As we integrate AI into these facets of life, we must strive to enhance rather than diminish the human experience. This involves fostering environments where AI complements human creativity and ingenuity, rather than replacing them.

Ultimately, addressing the ethical dilemmas posed by AI requires a collaborative effort across disciplines and sectors. It calls for a commitment to ethical principles that prioritize human dignity and societal well-being. By engaging with these challenges thoughtfully and proactively, we can harness the potential of AI to create a future where technology and humanity coexist harmoniously, driving progress without compromising our core values.

Guiding Principles

In envisioning the future of AI and human collaboration, a set of guiding principles emerges, designed to navigate this intricate relationship. Central to this is the understanding that AI should not be perceived as a mere tool but as a partner in progress. This partnership calls for a mindset shift, where AI is integrated into our lives in a way that respects and enhances human capabilities rather than replacing them. The synergy of AI and human intelligence should be cultivated through a framework that prioritizes ethical considerations, creative exploration, and continuous adaptation.

The first principle is the humanization of AI, which involves imbuing technology with values that reflect our collective aspirations and ethical standards. This means AI systems should be designed and implemented with a strong ethical foundation, ensuring that they operate transparently and accountably. Developers and users alike must engage in ongoing dialogue about the moral implications of AI, fostering environments where ethical AI can thrive.

Adapting to the rapid advancements in AI technology is another crucial principle. As AI continues to evolve, so too must our approaches to learning and skill development. This requires a commitment to lifelong learning, where individuals are encouraged to continuously update their knowledge and skills to keep pace with technological changes. Educational systems must evolve to prepare future generations for a world where AI is ubiquitous, emphasizing critical thinking and adaptability.

The principle of resonance highlights the importance of creating AI technologies that align with human needs and societal goals. AI should be developed with a focus on enhancing human experiences and solving real-world problems, from healthcare to environmental sustainability. By ensuring that AI resonates with human values, we can harness its potential to improve lives and address global challenges.

Finally, the transformation principle underscores the profound impact AI can have on society. AI has the potential to drive significant progress across various domains, but this requires a careful balance between technological advancement and human well-being. It is imperative to foster partnerships that promote innovation while safeguarding against potential risks and unintended consequences.

These guiding principles serve as a roadmap for navigating the future of AI and human collaboration. They emphasize the need for a thoughtful and balanced approach, where AI is not simply integrated into society, but is done so in a manner that respects and enhances human potential. By adhering to these principles, we can create a future where AI and humanity coexist harmoniously, driving collective progress and unlocking new possibilities.

Future Ethics

In the unfolding narrative of our interconnected world, the ethical dimensions of artificial intelligence (AI) emerge as a pivotal theme. This exploration invites us to ponder not just the technological advancements AI brings, but the profound ethical questions it raises. As AI systems become increasingly autonomous and ingrained in our daily lives, the responsibility to guide their evolution ethically becomes paramount.

The synergy between AI and human potential hinges on our ability to navigate this ethical landscape with clarity and foresight. The HEART framework—Humanize, Evaluate, Adapt, Resonate, and Transform—serves as a compass in this journey, emphasizing the need for a balanced approach where AI complements human values and intentions. Humanizing AI involves imbuing these systems with empathy, ensuring they reflect the diverse tapestry of human experiences and cultures. This requires a conscientious effort to involve diverse voices in the development process, mitigating biases that might otherwise proliferate unchecked.

Evaluating AI within an ethical framework demands a rigorous examination of both the benefits and potential harms. This involves a critical analysis of AI's impact across various sectors, from healthcare to finance, where the stakes are high and the implications profound. By anticipating the risks and vulnerabilities inherent in AI systems, we can create safeguards that protect against misuse and unintended consequences.

Adapting to the ethical challenges posed by AI necessitates a dynamic approach, one that embraces lifelong learning and flexibility. As AI technologies evolve, so too must our ethical frameworks and regulatory measures. This adaptability ensures that ethics remain at the forefront of AI innovation, guiding its trajectory in ways that enhance human dignity and societal well-being.

Resonating with the ethical implications of AI means fostering a collective consciousness that prioritizes transparency and accountability. This involves open dialogues between technologists, policymakers, and the public, creating an ecosystem where ethical considerations are integral to AI's developmental narrative. By cultivating trust and understanding, we pave the way for AI to be perceived not as a threat but as a collaborative partner in progress.

Transforming our ethical approach to AI involves reimagining the future with a mindset that embraces both caution and optimism. This transformation is not merely about avoiding harm but actively seeking ways AI can contribute to a more equitable and just society. It challenges us to envision AI as a catalyst for positive change, driving innovations that align with our highest ethical standards.

As we stand on the cusp of a new era, the ethics of AI invite us to reflect deeply on the kind of future we wish to create. This reflection is not a solitary endeavor but a collective one, requiring the participation of all stakeholders in shaping a world where AI and humanity coexist harmoniously. The ethical path forward is one of synergy, where AI's capabilities are harnessed for the greater good, ensuring that technological progress is synonymous with human advancement.

Chapter 6: AI Challenges and Opportunities

Risk Evaluation

Evaluating the potential risks associated with AI requires a nuanced understanding of both its transformative power and the ethical considerations that underpin its deployment. At the heart of this evaluation lies the need to balance innovation with responsibility, ensuring that AI serves as a tool for progress rather than a catalyst for harm. The process begins with acknowledging the dual nature of AI: it holds the promise of unprecedented advancements in fields such as healthcare, finance, and education, yet it also poses significant risks if not managed with care. These risks range from privacy violations and algorithmic biases to the displacement of jobs and the erosion of human agency.

To navigate these challenges, it is essential to adopt a comprehensive framework that emphasizes ethical considerations and stakeholder engagement. This involves assessing the societal impact of AI applications and fostering transparency in AI decision-making processes. By doing so, we can mitigate potential harms and promote a culture of accountability among AI developers and users.

Moreover, risk evaluation in the context of AI is not a static endeavor. It requires continuous monitoring and adaptation as technologies evolve and new use cases emerge. This dynamic approach ensures that we remain vigilant to emerging threats and opportunities, enabling us to respond effectively to the shifting landscape of AI innovation.

Collaboration between diverse stakeholders is also crucial in this evaluation process. Policymakers, technologists, ethicists, and the public must work together to establish guidelines and regulations that safeguard against the misuse of AI. By fostering an inclusive dialogue, we can ensure that the development and deployment of AI technologies align with societal values and priorities.

In addition to regulatory measures, fostering a culture of ethical AI development within organizations is paramount. This involves embedding ethical considerations into the design and implementation of AI systems, promoting diversity in AI teams, and encouraging a mindset of lifelong learning among AI practitioners. By cultivating these principles, we can create AI systems that are not only innovative but also aligned with the broader goals of human flourishing and societal well-being.

Ultimately, the evaluation of AI risks is a critical component of the broader effort to harness AI's potential while safeguarding against its pitfalls. By approaching this task with a thoughtful and proactive mindset, we can pave the way for a future where AI acts as a force for good, enhancing human capabilities and contributing to a more equitable and sustainable world.

Opportunity Maximization

In the evolving landscape where artificial intelligence intertwines with human existence, there lies a vast expanse of untapped potential waiting to be harnessed. The synergy between AI and human capabilities can be likened to a new frontier, brimming with opportunities that, when properly maximized, could redefine the essence of progress. This is not merely about leveraging technology for efficiency; it's about creating a harmonious partnership that enhances human creativity and innovation.

Consider the historical parallels that have shaped our understanding of technological advancements. Just as the

66

printing press democratized knowledge and the Industrial Revolution redefined labor, AI has the capability to transform how we approach problem-solving and creativity. It challenges us to rethink traditional paradigms and encourages the exploration of new possibilities that were once constrained by human limits.

The HEART framework serves as a guiding principle in this endeavor. By humanizing our interaction with AI, we ensure that technology serves to enhance rather than overshadow human potential. This involves evaluating the ethical implications and societal impacts of AI, fostering an environment where technology operates as an ally to humanity. Adapting to AI's rapid evolution requires a mindset of continuous learning and openness to change, ensuring that we remain at the forefront of innovation rather than becoming passive observers.

Resonating with AI's capabilities involves tapping into its potential to augment human creativity. By integrating AI into our daily workflows, we can unlock new levels of efficiency and insight, allowing for a more profound exploration of our creative faculties. This symbiotic relationship between human intuition and machine precision can lead to transformative outcomes, driving progress in ways previously unimaginable.

Transforming this potential into reality requires a collective effort from leaders, technologists, and policymakers. It's about creating an ecosystem where AI-human collaboration thrives, fostering an environment of innovation and ethical responsibility. By embracing this collaborative mindset, we pave the way for a future where technology and humanity coexist in harmony, each enhancing the other in a dance of mutual benefit.

The journey towards maximizing opportunities in the AI-human synergy is not without its challenges. It demands a reevaluation of our values, a commitment to ethical standards, and a willingness to explore uncharted territories. However, the rewards of such an endeavor are vast, offering the promise of a future where technology amplifies human potential rather than diminishing it.

As we stand on the cusp of this new era, it is imperative to approach AI with a mindset of possibility rather than limitation. By maximizing the opportunities presented by this powerful alliance, we have the chance to redefine the boundaries of human achievement, crafting a narrative where AI is not just a tool, but a partner in our collective evolution.

Challenge Mitigation

In the ever-evolving landscape of artificial intelligence, the challenges that arise are as diverse as they are complex. To navigate this terrain, one must adopt a mindset that is both flexible and forward-thinking, embracing the potential of AI while remaining vigilant to its pitfalls. The synergy between human intuition and machine efficiency can drive unprecedented progress, yet it requires a deliberate and thoughtful approach to mitigate the inherent challenges.

One of the primary challenges is the ethical implications of AI deployment. As AI systems become more integrated into our daily lives, they wield significant influence over decision-making processes, from healthcare diagnostics to financial predictions. Ensuring that these systems operate within an ethical framework is paramount. This involves not only programming ethical considerations into AI algorithms but also fostering a culture of accountability and transparency among developers and users alike. By prioritizing ethical standards, we can prevent the misuse of

AI technologies and protect against biases that may lead to unfair outcomes.

Another significant challenge is the potential for AI to disrupt labor markets. Automation and AI-driven processes can lead to job displacement, particularly in sectors reliant on routine tasks. However, this challenge can be mitigated by viewing AI as a tool for augmentation rather than replacement. By reskilling and upskilling the workforce, we can empower individuals to work alongside AI, leveraging its capabilities to enhance productivity and creativity. Educational initiatives must be implemented to equip workers with the necessary skills to thrive in an AI-enhanced economy, fostering adaptability and lifelong learning.

Data privacy is another area of concern. The vast amounts of data required to train AI systems pose risks to individual privacy and security. To mitigate these risks, robust data protection measures must be implemented. This includes the development of advanced encryption technologies, anonymization techniques, and stringent data governance policies. By prioritizing data privacy, we can build trust in AI systems and ensure that their benefits are realized without compromising personal freedoms.

Furthermore, the rapid pace of AI development presents a challenge in itself. Keeping up with technological advancements requires a dynamic approach to regulation and policy-making. Policymakers must work collaboratively with technologists and industry leaders to create adaptive regulatory frameworks that can evolve alongside AI innovations. This collaborative approach ensures that regulations do not stifle innovation but instead provide a safe and structured environment for AI to flourish.

Finally, fostering interdisciplinary collaboration is crucial in addressing the multifaceted challenges of AI. By bringing together experts from diverse fields—such as computer science, ethics, law, and social sciences—we can develop holistic solutions that address the technical, ethical, and societal implications of AI. This collaborative effort enables us to harness the full potential of AI, driving progress while safeguarding human values.

In conclusion, the challenges posed by AI are not insurmountable. By adopting a proactive and reflective mindset, we can mitigate these challenges and unlock the transformative potential of AI-human collaboration. This requires a commitment to ethical standards, continuous learning, data privacy, adaptive regulation, and interdisciplinary collaboration. Through these efforts, we can shape a future where AI serves as a catalyst for human advancement, driving progress in a manner that is both responsible and equitable.

Future Speculations

As we peer into the horizon of AI and human collaboration, the landscape is both exhilarating and complex, filled with opportunities that challenge our existing paradigms. The future beckons us to rethink our roles not just as creators or users of technology, but as integral partners in a symbiotic relationship with AI. This requires a shift in mindset, one that embraces the potential of AI to enhance human capabilities while maintaining a vigilant eye on ethical considerations.

The synergy between AI and humans opens up a plethora of possibilities. Imagine a world where AI-driven insights lead to breakthroughs in medicine, allowing for personalized treatment plans that evolve in real-time, guided by constant learning from global health data. Such advancements hold the promise of not only prolonging life but also improving its quality. However, this future demands careful navigation to ensure that the benefits of

AI are equitably distributed, avoiding the pitfalls of exacerbating existing inequalities.

In the realm of education, AI can transform how we learn, offering personalized learning experiences that adapt to individual needs and pace. This could democratize education, providing access to quality learning resources to those in remote or underserved areas. Yet, the challenge lies in maintaining the human elements of empathy, mentorship, and critical thinking, which are essential to a holistic educational experience.

The workplace, too, stands on the brink of transformation. AI can automate routine tasks, freeing humans to engage in more creative and strategic endeavors. This shift could lead to a renaissance in workplace innovation, where human ingenuity is amplified by AI capabilities. However, this transition necessitates a reimagining of workforce development, focusing on skills that complement AI, such as emotional intelligence and complex problem-solving.

Ethical considerations must remain at the forefront of AI development. As AI systems become more autonomous, questions of accountability, transparency, and bias become increasingly critical. It is imperative that we establish robust frameworks to govern AI, ensuring that it operates within boundaries that reflect our shared values. This requires a concerted effort from policymakers, technologists, and society at large to engage in continuous dialogue and reflection.

Looking ahead, the potential for AI to act as a catalyst for societal progress is immense. By fostering a collaborative mindset, we can harness AI to address global challenges such as climate change, poverty, and health crises. This vision of the future is not without its challenges, but with deliberate action and thoughtful leadership, we can steer the course towards a future where AI and humans coexist harmoniously, each enhancing the other's capabilities.

In this unfolding narrative, the role of humans is not diminished but rather elevated. By embracing AI as a partner, we stand to unlock new dimensions of creativity, understanding, and achievement. The journey towards this future requires courage, innovation, and a steadfast commitment to ethical principles, ensuring that the synergy between AI and humanity leads to a prosperous and equitable world for all.

Chapter 7: The Future of Work

AI in the Workplace

In the evolving landscape of contemporary work environments, artificial intelligence emerges not as a mere tool, but as a profound collaborator reshaping the very essence of productivity and creativity. The integration of AI into the workplace heralds a transformative era where human ingenuity finds an ally in machine precision and efficiency. This partnership offers a dynamic interplay where AI handles repetitive tasks, allowing humans to focus on strategic, creative, and interpersonal responsibilities.

Reflective of this synergy, workplaces are witnessing a paradigm shift. Traditional roles are being redefined, with AI taking over data-driven tasks, thus freeing employees to engage in more meaningful work that requires emotional intelligence and critical thinking. This transition demands a new skill set, urging professionals to adapt swiftly to harness AI's potential fully. It is not just about learning how to use AI tools but understanding how to collaborate with these systems to enhance decision-making processes and innovate solutions.

The integration of AI also brings about a democratization of skills. With AI-powered tools, employees at all levels can access insights and analytics that were once the domain of specialized experts. This accessibility fosters a more inclusive environment where diverse perspectives can converge to drive innovation. Moreover, AI's ability to process vast amounts of data quickly and accurately supports more informed decision-making, reducing the margin of error and enhancing the quality of outcomes.

However, this integration is not without its challenges. Ethical considerations loom large as AI systems become more autonomous. The responsibility lies in ensuring these systems are designed and deployed in ways that uphold fairness, transparency, and accountability. Organizations must cultivate a culture of continuous learning and adaptation, preparing their workforce to navigate the ethical complexities that accompany AI technologies.

Furthermore, the psychological impact of AI in the workplace cannot be overlooked. As AI systems become more prevalent, there is a need to address potential anxieties and resistance among employees. Building trust in AI systems is crucial, which can be achieved through transparent communication and by involving employees in the AI integration process. Empowering employees with knowledge about AI's capabilities and limitations can mitigate fears and foster a more collaborative atmosphere.

The future of work, augmented by AI, promises unprecedented opportunities for growth and innovation. By embracing AI as a partner, organizations can unlock new levels of efficiency and creativity, setting the stage for a future where human potential is amplified rather than diminished. This collaborative approach not only enhances productivity but also enriches the human experience at work, paving the way for a more fulfilling and balanced professional life.

Ultimately, the successful integration of AI in the workplace hinges on a balanced approach that respects human values and leverages technological advancements. By fostering a culture of collaboration, continuous learning, and ethical responsibility, organizations can navigate the complexities of AI integration and emerge as leaders in the new era of work.

Job Evolution

Reflecting upon the history of work, one observes how the advent of technology has consistently reshaped the landscape of employment. From the mechanization of the Industrial Revolution to the digital transformation of the Information Age, each era has introduced tools that have redefined roles, responsibilities, and even the concept of work itself. Today, we stand on the brink of another monumental shift, driven by artificial intelligence (AI), which promises not just to change how we work, but to revolutionize what work can be.

AI's integration into the workforce is not merely an incremental upgrade; it represents a fundamental rethinking of human potential. Unlike previous technological advancements that primarily enhanced physical capabilities, AI amplifies cognitive functions, offering unprecedented opportunities for augmentation rather than replacement. This distinction is crucial as it repositions AI as a collaborator, not a competitor. The synergy between human creativity and AI's analytical prowess can lead to innovations that neither could achieve alone.

In considering the evolution of jobs, one must recognize the shift from routine, rule-based tasks to those requiring emotional intelligence, critical thinking, and complex problem-solving. As AI takes on more of the repetitive and data-intensive tasks, humans are liberated to focus on areas where they excel – empathy, creativity, and strategic decision-making. This transition necessitates a reimagining of education and training, emphasizing lifelong learning and adaptability. The future workforce will need to cultivate skills that complement AI technologies, fostering a partnership where both entities enhance each other's strengths.

Moreover, the transformation of jobs through AI invites a reevaluation of organizational structures and cultures. Companies are encouraged to adopt a mindset that values flexibility and innovation, where hierarchical models give way to more collaborative, networked approaches. This cultural shift not only supports the integration of AI but also empowers employees to take initiative and drive change from within. The ability to navigate and manage this new dynamic will be a defining factor for successful organizations in the AI era.

The potential of AI to democratize access to information and resources further accentuates its role in job evolution. By breaking down barriers and enabling global connectivity, AI can facilitate more equitable opportunities across different regions and demographics. This democratization is poised to unlock human potential on a scale previously unimaginable, fostering a more inclusive and diverse workforce.

As we look toward the future, it is imperative to address the ethical considerations inherent in AI's impact on jobs. Ensuring that AI is developed and deployed responsibly involves a commitment to transparency, fairness, and accountability. Policymakers, technologists, and business leaders must collaborate to create frameworks that protect workers' rights and promote social welfare. By doing so, we can harness AI's transformative power to build a future where technology enhances human life without compromising dignity or equity.

The evolution of jobs in the AI age is a testament to the enduring adaptability and resilience of the human spirit. By embracing AI as a partner in progress, we can redefine work in ways that enhance human potential and contribute to a more prosperous and harmonious society.

Collaboration Techniques

In the dynamic landscape of technological advancement, the convergence of artificial intelligence (AI) and human capabilities offers unprecedented opportunities for collaboration. This synergy is not only desirable but essential for navigating the complexities of the modern world. The HEART framework provides a structured approach to fostering this collaboration, emphasizing the importance of human creativity, ethical considerations, and adaptive learning in the integration of AI into our daily lives.

At the core of successful collaboration between AI and humans lies the ability to humanize technology, ensuring that AI systems are designed with empathy and understanding. This involves creating interfaces that are intuitive and user-friendly, allowing individuals to interact with AI in a manner that feels natural and supportive. By prioritizing the human experience, we can build trust and facilitate a more seamless integration of AI into various aspects of life.

Evaluation plays a critical role in collaboration, as it requires a thorough assessment of the risks and benefits associated with AI. This involves not only understanding the technical capabilities of AI systems but also considering their potential impact on society. By evaluating AI through a lens of ethical responsibility, we can identify opportunities to leverage technology for the greater good while mitigating potential harms. This balanced approach ensures that AI serves as a tool for empowerment rather than a source of division.

Adaptation is another key element in the collaborative process, as it enables both individuals and organizations to keep pace with the rapid evolution of AI technology. This requires a commitment to lifelong learning and the development of skills that complement AI capabilities. By embracing change and fostering a culture of continuous improvement, we can ensure that humans remain at the forefront of innovation, guiding the development of AI in a direction that aligns with our values and aspirations.

Resonance, the ability to align AI initiatives with human goals and values, is crucial for creating meaningful partnerships. This involves a deep understanding of the needs and desires of individuals, as well as the broader societal context in which AI operates. By ensuring that AI initiatives resonate with human priorities, we can drive progress that is both sustainable and inclusive, fostering a future where technology enhances rather than detracts from the human experience.

Transformation, the final component of the HEART framework, emphasizes the transformative potential of AI-human collaboration. By harnessing the complementary strengths of AI and humans, we can unlock new possibilities for innovation and creativity. This transformation is not about replacing human capabilities with technology but rather augmenting them, creating new pathways for growth and development. Through collaboration, we can shape a future that is not only technologically advanced but also deeply human, characterized by empathy, understanding, and shared purpose.

Workplace Transformation

In a world where technology is rapidly evolving, the workplace finds itself at a pivotal crossroads. The integration of artificial intelligence into our professional environments is not merely a trend but a transformative force reshaping how we perceive work and productivity. The synergy between AI and human capabilities is redefining roles, responsibilities, and the very essence of work itself. This transformation, however, is not without its challenges and opportunities. It requires a reimagining of workplace dynamics, where AI acts as a collaborator, enhancing human potential rather than replacing it. This subchapter delves into the nuances of this transformation, exploring the profound impact AI is having on the workplace, and how organizations can navigate this shift responsibly and effectively.

The first aspect of workplace transformation is the shift in job roles. As AI takes over repetitive and mundane tasks, it frees humans to focus on more complex, creative, and strategic functions. This shift necessitates a reevaluation of skills and competencies required in the modern workplace. Organizations must invest in upskilling and reskilling their workforce to ensure that employees can thrive in an AI-augmented environment. This not only enhances productivity but also fosters a culture of continuous learning and innovation.

Moreover, AI's integration into the workplace introduces new ethical considerations. Organizations must ensure that AI systems are designed and implemented with fairness, transparency, and accountability. This involves establishing clear guidelines and frameworks that govern the use of AI, protecting employee rights, and ensuring that AI-driven decisions do not perpetuate biases. It is crucial for businesses to engage in open dialogues with employees, stakeholders, and the public to build trust and acceptance of AI technologies.

The transformation is also reshaping organizational structures and cultures. Traditional hierarchical models are giving way to more agile and flexible structures that encourage collaboration and cross-functional teams. AI tools facilitate seamless communication and information sharing, breaking down silos and enabling more efficient workflows. This fosters a more inclusive and diverse workplace, where diverse perspectives are valued and integrated into decision-making processes.

Furthermore, AI is driving innovation by enabling new ways of working and creating value. From predictive analytics that drive strategic decision-making to automation that enhances operational efficiency, AI is unlocking new opportunities for growth and competitiveness. Organizations that embrace this transformation are better positioned to adapt to changing market demands and customer expectations. However, this requires a mindset shift, where leaders champion AI adoption and encourage a culture of experimentation and risk-taking.

Ultimately, the workplace transformation driven by AI is not just about technology; it is about people. It is about creating environments where humans and machines collaborate harmoniously, leveraging each other's strengths to achieve common goals. This requires a holistic approach that balances technological advancements with human values, ensuring that the transformation benefits all stakeholders. By embracing AI as a partner, organizations can unlock new possibilities and drive sustainable growth in the digital age.

Chapter 8: Learning in the AI Era

Educational Paradigms

In a world where artificial intelligence is rapidly becoming an integral part of everyday life, it is crucial to reimagine how education can evolve to prepare individuals for this new era. The traditional educational paradigms, deeply rooted in rote learning and standardized testing, may no longer suffice in a landscape that demands creativity, critical thinking, and adaptability. The synergy between AI and human capabilities offers a transformative opportunity to redefine educational frameworks, enabling learners to thrive in an AI-enhanced future.

At the heart of this transformation is the need to cultivate a mindset that embraces both human and artificial intelligence as complementary forces. This involves fostering an environment where students are encouraged to explore and experiment, rather than merely absorb information. By leveraging AI technologies, educators can create personalized learning experiences that cater to the unique needs and interests of each student, thereby nurturing their innate curiosity and passion for discovery.

Moreover, the integration of AI in education calls for a shift from traditional teacher-centered approaches to more collaborative and interactive learning models. Educators must become facilitators of knowledge, guiding students in navigating complex problems and developing solutions through teamwork and innovation. AI can play a pivotal role in this process by providing real-time feedback, analyzing learning patterns, and offering insights that help students refine their understanding and skills.

Ethical considerations are also paramount in the evolving educational landscape. As AI becomes more embedded in learning environments, it is essential to instill values of responsibility, empathy, and ethical decision-making in students. This can be achieved by incorporating discussions on AI ethics, data privacy, and the societal impact of technology into the curriculum, ensuring that learners are equipped to use AI responsibly and ethically.

Furthermore, the rapid evolution of AI necessitates a commitment to lifelong learning. Educational paradigms must adapt to prepare individuals not only for the jobs of today but also for those of tomorrow, many of which may not yet exist. This requires a focus on developing skills such as adaptability, resilience, and continuous learning, empowering students to remain agile in the face of change.

In this new educational paradigm, the role of AI is not to replace human educators but to augment their capabilities, enabling them to focus on what they do best: inspiring and mentoring students. By harnessing the power of AI, educators can free up time to engage in meaningful interactions with students, fostering a deeper understanding and appreciation of the world around them.

The synergy between AI and education holds the promise of unlocking human potential in unprecedented ways. As we navigate this transformative journey, it is crucial to remain mindful of the values and principles that define us as human beings, ensuring that technology serves as a tool for empowerment and growth. Through thoughtful integration of AI into educational paradigms, we can pave the way for a future where learners are equipped not only with knowledge but with the wisdom to shape a better world.

AI in Education

In the ever-evolving landscape of education, AI has emerged as a powerful tool that holds the potential to revolutionize learning experiences. As educators and learners navigate this new terrain, it becomes increasingly clear that AI is not just a technological advancement but a catalyst for reimagining educational paradigms. The integration of AI into educational settings offers opportunities to enhance personalized learning, streamline administrative tasks, and expand access to knowledge, thus fostering an environment where every learner can thrive.

AI's role in personalizing education cannot be overstated. By analyzing vast amounts of data, AI systems can tailor educational content to meet the unique needs of individual students. This personalization extends beyond mere content delivery; it encompasses pacing, learning styles, and even the emotional state of learners. For instance, adaptive learning platforms use AI algorithms to identify areas where a student may struggle and subsequently adjust the curriculum to bridge these gaps. This dynamic approach not only enhances understanding but also boosts student confidence and motivation.

Moreover, AI can alleviate the administrative burdens that often detract from teaching and learning. By automating routine tasks such as grading, scheduling, and resource allocation, educators can focus more on facilitating meaningful interactions with students. This shift allows teachers to adopt more innovative pedagogical strategies and dedicate their time to fostering critical thinking and creativity in their classrooms. In essence, AI acts as an enabler, freeing educators to concentrate on what they do best: inspire and engage learners.

Accessibility is another domain where AI's impact is profound. With AI-driven tools, educational resources can be made available to a broader audience, including those with disabilities or those who reside in remote areas. Speech recognition, text-to-speech, and real-time translation services are just a few examples of how AI is breaking down barriers to education. These technologies ensure that learning is inclusive and equitable, providing every individual with the opportunity to access quality education regardless of their circumstances.

However, the integration of AI in education also presents challenges, particularly concerning data privacy and the ethical use of AI systems. As educational institutions collect more data to facilitate personalized learning, they must also ensure that this data is protected and used responsibly.

Educators and policymakers must work together to establish guidelines that safeguard student information while allowing the benefits of AI to be fully realized.

Ultimately, the successful incorporation of AI in education hinges on a collaborative effort between technology developers, educators, and policymakers. By working together, these stakeholders can create a learning environment that is not only technologically advanced but also deeply human-centered. This synergy will pave the way for a future where education is more engaging, inclusive, and effective, preparing learners to thrive in an increasingly complex world. As AI continues to evolve, so too must our approaches to education, ensuring that technology serves as a bridge to greater understanding and opportunity for all.

Adaptive Learning

In the rapidly evolving landscape of artificial intelligence, the concept of adaptive learning emerges as a keystone for both individuals and organizations striving to thrive amidst the technological revolution. Adaptive learning is more than just an educational tool; it represents a paradigm shift in how we approach knowledge acquisition and skill development in an AI-driven world. This subchapter delves into the essence of adaptive learning, exploring its transformative potential and the ways it can be harnessed to foster a more synergistic relationship between humans and machines.

At its core, adaptive learning leverages AI to tailor educational experiences to the unique needs of each learner. This personalized approach stands in stark contrast to traditional, one-size-fits-all educational models, which often fail to address the diverse learning styles and paces of individuals. By utilizing algorithms that analyze data on a learner's performance, preferences, and progress, adaptive learning systems can dynamically adjust content, difficulty levels, and instructional strategies. This ensures that each learner receives the optimal support needed to achieve their fullest potential.

The benefits of adaptive learning extend beyond individual empowerment. In a broader sense, it serves as a catalyst for organizational innovation and agility. Companies that embrace adaptive learning technologies can cultivate a workforce that is not only more skilled but also more resilient to change. In a business environment where technological advancements are constant, the ability to quickly acquire and apply new skills is invaluable. Adaptive learning provides a framework for ongoing professional development, enabling employees to continually update their competencies in alignment with emerging industry trends and demands.

Moreover, adaptive learning plays a crucial role in bridging the digital divide. By making education more accessible and inclusive, it can democratize learning opportunities for people from diverse backgrounds and geographies. This inclusivity is essential in ensuring that the benefits of AI and technological progress are distributed equitably across society. As adaptive learning systems become more sophisticated, they have the potential to reach underserved populations, offering tailored educational experiences that were previously unattainable.

However, the implementation of adaptive learning is not without challenges. Issues of data privacy and security must be carefully managed to protect learners' sensitive information. Additionally, there is a need for ongoing research and development to refine adaptive learning technologies, ensuring they are effective, equitable, and aligned with educational goals. Stakeholders, including educators, technologists, and policymakers, must collaborate to create frameworks that support the ethical and responsible use of adaptive learning.

As we look to the future, adaptive learning stands as a beacon of what is possible when AI is integrated thoughtfully into the fabric of education and professional development. It exemplifies the potential for AI to enhance, rather than replace, human capabilities. By fostering a culture of continuous learning and adaptability, we can prepare individuals and organizations to navigate the complexities of the AI era with confidence and creativity. In doing so, we not only embrace the transformative power of AI but also reaffirm our commitment to a future where technology and humanity advance hand in hand.

Future Learning Models

As we delve into the evolving landscape of education and learning, the synergy between artificial intelligence and human intellect becomes a focal point. The future learning models are poised to transcend traditional boundaries, integrating AI to create an adaptive, personalized, and more efficient educational experience. This transformation is not merely about implementing new technologies but reimagining the entire educational paradigm to foster a more inclusive and dynamic learning environment.

In these emerging models, AI serves as both a tool and a partner in the educational journey. It enables a level of personalization previously unattainable, tailoring educational content to meet the unique needs, pace, and style of each learner. Through sophisticated algorithms, AI can analyze vast amounts of data to identify learning patterns and predict future performance, offering insights that educators can use to enhance teaching methods and outcomes.

The role of AI in education extends beyond personalization. It acts as a catalyst for lifelong learning, encouraging learners to continuously adapt and acquire new skills in response to the ever-changing demands of the modern world. By integrating AI into learning systems, educational institutions can offer courses that evolve in real-time, ensuring that the curriculum remains relevant and aligned with industry advancements.

Moreover, AI facilitates a more collaborative learning environment. Virtual classrooms and AI-driven platforms enable learners from diverse backgrounds to connect and collaborate, breaking down geographical and cultural barriers. This interconnectedness enriches the learning experience, fostering a global perspective and promoting cultural understanding.

However, the integration of AI in education also presents challenges that must be addressed to ensure equitable access and prevent the exacerbation of existing educational disparities. It is crucial to implement ethical guidelines and frameworks that govern the use of AI in education, ensuring that the technology is used responsibly and inclusively. Educators and policymakers must work together to develop strategies that mitigate potential biases in AI systems and ensure that all learners benefit equally from these advancements.

Furthermore, the role of educators is evolving in this new landscape. Rather than being the sole providers of knowledge, educators become facilitators and guides, helping students navigate the wealth of information available through AI-powered tools. This shift requires a new set of skills and competencies, highlighting the importance of professional development and training for educators to effectively integrate AI into their teaching practices.

In conclusion, the future of learning models is a harmonious blend of AI and human creativity, where technology enhances the educational experience without overshadowing the essential human elements of empathy, critical thinking, and ethical reasoning. By embracing this synergy, we can create a learning environment that not only prepares individuals for the workforce but also cultivates a more thoughtful, innovative, and inclusive society. As we move forward, it is imperative to approach this transformation with a balanced perspective, ensuring that the benefits of AI in education are realized while maintaining the core values of humanity and learning.

Chapter 9: Creativity and Innovation

Creative AI

The integration of artificial intelligence into the creative process marks a revolutionary shift in how we perceive and engage with creativity itself. This transformation is not merely about enhancing efficiency but about redefining the boundaries of human imagination and innovation. As AI systems become more adept at generating art, music, and literature, they challenge us to reconsider the essence of creativity and the role of human agency in the creative process.

In the past, creativity was seen as an exclusively human trait, a mysterious force that could not be replicated by machines. However, the advent of AI has begun to blur these lines, introducing new forms of creativity that are collaborative rather than solitary. AI acts as a creative partner, offering novel ideas and perspectives that might not occur to a human mind. This partnership can lead to extraordinary outcomes, as AI's ability to process vast amounts of data and identify patterns complements human intuition and emotional depth.

One of the key aspects of creative AI is its ability to democratize the creative process. By providing tools that are accessible to a broader audience, AI enables individuals who may not have traditional artistic skills to express themselves creatively. This democratization of creativity fosters inclusivity and diversity, allowing for a richer tapestry of cultural expression. Moreover, AI-driven platforms can facilitate collaboration across geographical and cultural boundaries, leading to a more interconnected and harmonious global creative community.

However, the rise of creative AI also brings forth ethical considerations that must be addressed. As AI systems generate content that mimics human creativity, questions about authorship and originality arise. It is essential to establish frameworks that recognize and protect the rights of both human and AI contributors. Additionally, the potential for AI to perpetuate biases present in its training data necessitates a vigilant approach to its development and deployment. By ensuring that AI is used responsibly, we can harness its potential to enhance, rather than diminish, the richness of human creativity.

The synergy between human creativity and AI is not a threat to the artist but an opportunity for expansion. By embracing AI as a collaborator, artists can explore new realms of possibility, pushing the boundaries of what can be achieved in the arts. This collaborative mindset requires an openness to experimentation and a willingness to learn from the machine as much as the machine learns from us.

As we stand on the cusp of this new era, it is crucial to cultivate a mindset that values both human and artificial contributions. By doing so, we can create a future where creativity is not limited by human constraints but is instead amplified by the limitless possibilities that AI offers. This synergy between human and machine creativity promises to usher in a new Renaissance, where technology serves as a catalyst for human expression, innovation, and cultural evolution.

Innovation Catalysts

In the ever-evolving landscape of artificial intelligence, the role of innovation catalysts becomes pivotal. These catalysts act as bridges, connecting the realms of human creativity and machine efficiency. They are the visionaries who perceive AI not as a mere tool, but as a partner in the quest for progress. This partnership is rooted in a deep understanding of the potential that lies in the synergy of human ingenuity and AI capabilities.

Reflecting on historical precedents, one can draw parallels to the transformative power of the printing press or the industrial revolution. These innovations were not merely technological advancements; they were catalysts that reshaped societies, economies, and cultures. Similarly, today's innovation catalysts in the AI domain strive to harness this revolutionary potential to drive substantial societal change. They are the ones who see beyond the immediate applications of AI, envisioning a future where AI amplifies human potential rather than replacing it.

The catalysts of innovation are characterized by their ability to navigate the complexities of AI with a nuanced understanding of both its possibilities and limitations. They advocate for a mindful integration of AI into various sectors, ensuring that the deployment of AI technologies is aligned with ethical standards and human values. This requires a balance between embracing technological advancements and safeguarding the essence of humanity.

Moreover, these catalysts are often at the forefront of interdisciplinary collaborations, bringing together experts from diverse fields to foster innovation. They understand that the challenges posed by AI are multifaceted and require a holistic approach. By facilitating dialogues between technologists, ethicists, policymakers, and the public, they lay the groundwork for responsible AI development. This collaborative mindset is essential for creating AI systems that are not only efficient but also equitable and inclusive.

The role of innovation catalysts extends beyond mere advocacy and collaboration. They are also educators, raising awareness about the implications of AI and empowering individuals to engage with AI technologies critically. Through workshops, seminars, and public discussions, they demystify AI, making it accessible to a broader audience. This educational aspect is crucial, as it equips individuals with the knowledge and skills necessary to navigate an AI-driven world.

As AI continues to evolve, the challenges it presents will become increasingly complex. However, with innovation catalysts leading the way, there is hope for a future where AI and humanity coexist harmoniously. These catalysts remind us that at the heart of AI innovation is the human spirit—curious, resilient, and ever-aspiring to push the boundaries of what is possible. By fostering an environment that encourages experimentation and creativity, they ensure that AI remains a force for good, driving progress and enhancing the human experience.

In this light, the role of innovation catalysts is not just to spur technological advancement but to guide it in a direction that benefits all of humanity. They are the stewards of the AI revolution, ensuring that as we move forward, we do so with a sense of purpose, responsibility, and shared vision for a better future.

Creative Collaborations

In the evolving landscape of artificial intelligence, the potential for creative collaborations between humans and AI is not just a possibility but a necessity. The synergy that arises from combining human intuition and creativity with AI's analytical prowess can lead to unprecedented innovations. This partnership is akin to a dance, where each party brings its unique strengths to the table, enhancing the other's abilities.

AI, with its capacity to process vast amounts of data at lightning speed, offers insights that can fuel human creativity. It acts as a catalyst, inspiring new ideas and pushing the boundaries of what is possible. For instance, in the realm of art and design, AI can analyze patterns and trends, providing artists with new perspectives and techniques that they might not have considered. This collaboration does not diminish the artist's role but rather elevates it, allowing for the creation of works that are both innovative and deeply human.

In business, AI's role in creative collaborations is equally transformative. By handling routine tasks and analyzing complex data sets, AI frees up human workers to focus on more creative and strategic endeavors. This shift not only enhances productivity but also fosters a more fulfilling work environment where creativity is encouraged and valued. Companies that embrace this collaboration find themselves at the forefront of innovation, able to adapt quickly to changing market demands and consumer preferences.

Moreover, the educational sector stands to benefit immensely from AI-human collaborations. AI can personalize learning experiences, tailoring content to meet the needs of individual students. This personalized approach not only enhances learning outcomes but also inspires students to explore their creative potential. Educators, in turn, are empowered to focus on nurturing critical thinking and creativity, skills that are essential in the modern world.

The ethical dimension of these collaborations cannot be overlooked. As AI becomes more integrated into creative processes, it is crucial to ensure that these technologies are used responsibly. This involves fostering a culture of transparency and accountability, where the ethical implications of AI-driven decisions are carefully considered. By doing so, we can ensure that AI serves as a tool for empowerment rather than a source of division or inequality.

The future of creative collaborations between humans and AI is bright. As we continue to explore and refine these partnerships, we must remain committed to a vision of collaboration that is inclusive, ethical, and forward-thinking. By harnessing the unique strengths of both humans and AI, we can unlock new levels of creativity and innovation, paving the way for a future where technology and humanity coexist harmoniously.

Future of Creativity

In the ever-evolving landscape of creativity, the convergence of artificial intelligence and human ingenuity marks a significant milestone. This synergy is shaping a new frontier where creativity is not only enhanced but redefined. As AI systems become more sophisticated, they increasingly serve as catalysts for human creativity, sparking new ideas and pushing the boundaries of what is possible.

This transformation is not about AI replacing human creativity; rather, it is about AI augmenting and expanding our creative capabilities. AI tools can analyze vast amounts of data, identify patterns, and generate ideas that humans might not conceive independently. This collaboration allows creatives to explore uncharted territories, experiment with novel concepts, and innovate at an unprecedented pace.

The role of AI in creativity extends beyond mere assistance. It challenges us to rethink traditional creative processes and encourages a more collaborative approach. Artists, designers, and writers are now working alongside AI to co-create, leveraging the strengths of both human intuition and machine precision. This partnership fosters a dynamic creative environment where AI acts as both a muse and a collaborator.

Moreover, the integration of AI in creative fields prompts a reevaluation of authorship and originality. As AI-generated content becomes more prevalent, questions arise about the nature of creativity itself. Who owns the creations born from this collaboration? How do we define originality in a world where machines contribute to the creative process? These questions invite a deeper exploration of the ethics and values that underpin creative work.

In this brave new world, the HEART framework— Humanize, Evaluate, Adapt, Resonate, Transform— provides a roadmap for navigating the future of creativity. By humanizing AI, we ensure that technology serves to enhance human experiences rather than detract from them. Evaluating AI's impact on creativity involves a careful balance of embracing innovation while safeguarding the essence of human expression.

Adaptation is key as we learn to work alongside AI, cultivating a mindset that embraces lifelong learning and flexibility. Resonating with AI involves creating meaningful connections between human and machine, ensuring that our creative outputs reflect a harmonious blend of both. Finally, transformation occurs as we leverage AI to push the boundaries of what creativity can achieve, driving progress and innovation across all domains.

The future of creativity is a collaborative tapestry woven from the threads of human imagination and AI capability. This partnership holds the potential to unlock new realms of artistic expression, solve complex problems, and inspire a new generation of creators. As we stand on the cusp of this exciting era, it is imperative to approach the future with an open mind and a willingness to explore the limitless possibilities that arise when humans and AI create together.

Chapter 10: AI-Human Synergy

Partnership Dynamics

In the ever-evolving landscape of technology, the integration of artificial intelligence with human endeavors is not just a possibility but an imperative. This synergy between AI and humans is reshaping how we perceive partnerships, urging a reevaluation of traditional dynamics. As we navigate this transformative era, it's essential to understand that AI is not merely a tool but a collaborator that can enhance human potential in unprecedented ways.

The key to successful integration lies in embracing a mindset that views AI as a partner. This perspective shifts the narrative from competition to collaboration, fostering an environment where both entities complement each other. Humans bring creativity, empathy, and ethical considerations to the table, while AI contributes with speed, precision, and data-driven insights. Together, they form a partnership that is greater than the sum of its parts.

This collaborative approach necessitates a cultural shift within organizations. Leaders and teams must cultivate an openness to change and a willingness to learn. This involves not only adopting new technologies but also rethinking processes and workflows to integrate AI seamlessly. By doing so, organizations can unlock new levels of productivity and innovation, driving growth and competitiveness in a rapidly changing market.

Moreover, the partnership dynamics between AI and humans demand a focus on ethical considerations. As AI systems become more integrated into decision-making processes, ensuring they align with human values is crucial. This involves setting clear guidelines and frameworks that govern AI behavior, protecting against biases, and ensuring transparency. By prioritizing ethics, organizations can build trust with stakeholders and create a sustainable foundation for AI adoption.

The journey towards harmonious AI-human partnerships is also about empowerment. By leveraging AI, individuals can enhance their capabilities, expanding what is possible within their roles. AI can take over repetitive tasks, freeing up time for humans to focus on strategic and creative endeavors. This shift not only improves job satisfaction but also leads to more meaningful contributions to organizational goals.

In education and skill development, AI's role as a partner is equally transformative. It offers personalized learning experiences, adapting to individual needs and pacing, thus democratizing access to knowledge. This personalized approach empowers learners to acquire new skills and adapt to changing job landscapes, ensuring they remain relevant in a future dominated by technology.

In conclusion, the dynamics of AI-human partnerships are fundamentally reshaping the fabric of society. By fostering a collaborative mindset, prioritizing ethics, and embracing continuous learning, we can unlock the full potential of this synergy. The future is not about AI replacing humans but about creating a new paradigm where both thrive together, driving progress and innovation. As we stand on the brink of this new era, it is our responsibility to shape it thoughtfully, ensuring that AI serves humanity's best interests.

Synergistic Potential

In the unfolding narrative of AI and human collaboration, we find ourselves at a pivotal juncture where the potential for synergy is not just possible but imperative. This chapter delves into the profound possibilities that arise when artificial intelligence is integrated into human endeavors with a mindset geared toward collaboration rather than competition. Central to this exploration is the HEART Framework, which serves as a guide for fostering meaningful AI-human partnerships. At its core, this framework emphasizes the importance of humanizing AI interactions, ensuring that technology resonates with our values and aspirations.

The potential for synergy lies in the intersection of human creativity and AI's computational prowess. In fields ranging from healthcare to the arts, we witness AI's capacity to augment human capabilities, offering insights and efficiencies previously unimaginable. For instance, in healthcare, AI algorithms can analyze vast datasets to identify patterns and suggest treatments, supporting doctors in making more informed decisions. Meanwhile, in the arts, AI-powered tools allow artists to explore new dimensions of creativity, blurring the lines between human and machine-generated art.

However, unlocking this potential requires more than just technological integration. It demands a shift in mindset— one that embraces adaptability and lifelong learning. As AI continues to evolve, so too must our approaches to education and skill development. By fostering an environment of continuous learning, individuals can stay abreast of technological advancements, ensuring that they are not left behind in an increasingly digital world.

Equally important is the ethical dimension of AI integration. As we harness AI's capabilities, we must remain vigilant about the ethical implications of its use. This involves evaluating the risks and opportunities associated with AI applications, ensuring that they do not exacerbate existing inequalities or create new ethical dilemmas. By embedding ethical considerations into the development and deployment of AI technologies, we can create systems that not only enhance human potential but do so in a way that is fair and just.

The synergistic potential of AI and human collaboration also extends to the realm of innovation. By leveraging AI as a tool for innovation, industries can unlock new possibilities for growth and transformation. This is particularly evident in sectors such as finance and logistics, where AI-driven insights can optimize operations and drive strategic decision-making. Yet, to truly harness this potential, organizations must cultivate a culture that encourages experimentation and embraces the transformative power of AI.

Ultimately, the synergistic potential of AI and human collaboration is a testament to the power of partnership. By viewing AI as an ally rather than an adversary, we can unlock new avenues for human achievement and progress. This chapter calls upon leaders, technologists, and policymakers to embrace this potential, fostering environments where AI and human creativity can thrive together. Through thoughtful integration and ethical stewardship, we can shape a future where technology enhances, rather than diminishes, the human experience.

Mutual Growth

In the evolving landscape of technology, the partnership between humans and artificial intelligence presents a unique opportunity for mutual growth. This relationship is not merely about coexistence but about creating a dynamic synergy that propels both entities toward unprecedented realms of potential. The notion of mutual growth emphasizes a harmonious integration where human creativity, ethical considerations, and emotional intelligence are amplified by the computational prowess and precision of AI.

The essence of this collaboration lies in the recognition that both humans and AI bring distinct strengths to the table. Humans are inherently innovative, driven by curiosity and an innate ability to think abstractly and contextually. In contrast, AI excels in processing vast amounts of data with speed and accuracy, identifying patterns that might elude the human eye. By leveraging these complementary capabilities, we can address complex challenges across various sectors such as healthcare, education, and environmental sustainability.

Consider the transformative impact of AI in healthcare: AI systems can analyze medical data to predict disease outbreaks, assist in early diagnosis, and personalize treatment plans. This not only enhances the precision of medical interventions but also empowers healthcare professionals to focus more on patient care and empathy, aspects where human touch is irreplaceable. Similarly, in education, AI can tailor learning experiences to individual needs, allowing educators to devote more time to nurturing critical thinking and creativity.

Mutual growth also demands a shift in mindset. It requires an openness to continuous learning and adaptation from both parties. For humans, this means embracing AI not as a competitor but as a collaborator that can augment our abilities and extend our reach. For AI, this involves evolving from mere tools to partners that understand and respect human values and ethics. This evolution is guided by frameworks that prioritize ethical considerations, ensuring that AI development aligns with societal goals and human welfare.

The journey towards mutual growth is not without its challenges. It necessitates addressing ethical dilemmas and potential biases inherent in AI systems. It calls for robust governance structures that oversee AI's integration into society, ensuring transparency and accountability. Furthermore, it requires fostering an inclusive dialogue that encompasses diverse perspectives, ensuring that the benefits of AI are equitably distributed.

Ultimately, the path to mutual growth is a collaborative endeavor. It invites stakeholders from all walks of life—technologists, policymakers, educators, and the general public—to engage in a meaningful discourse about the future we want to create. By working together, we can harness the full potential of AI while safeguarding the core values that define our humanity.

In this new era, the synergy between AI and humans is not just a possibility; it is a necessity. It is a call to action to rethink and redefine our roles, not only in relation to technology but within the broader tapestry of life. As we navigate this transformative journey, let us strive to cultivate a partnership that is not only mutually beneficial but also deeply transformative, paving the way for a future where both AI and human potential flourish together.

Harmonious Future

Reflecting on the evolving landscape of technology and human interaction, we find ourselves at a pivotal moment where the convergence of AI and human potential creates an unprecedented opportunity for synergy. This future is not one of mere coexistence but of a harmonious partnership that transcends current boundaries, fostering a new era of innovation and understanding. In this vision, AI is not a mere tool, but a collaborative partner, enhancing human creativity, decision-making, and problem-solving abilities.

As we delve into this future, it is essential to focus on the principles of the HEART framework, which guides this transformative journey. The first tenet, Humanize, emphasizes the importance of embedding human values and ethics into AI systems. By ensuring that AI reflects our best qualities—empathy, kindness, and fairness—we cultivate technologies that support rather than undermine our humanity. This humanization of AI fosters trust and acceptance, paving the way for deeper integration into our lives.

Evaluating AI's impact is the next crucial step. This involves a balanced assessment of risks and opportunities, acknowledging that while AI can drive remarkable advancements, it also poses challenges that must be addressed responsibly. Through rigorous evaluation, we can identify and mitigate potential harms while maximizing the benefits of AI in various sectors, from healthcare to education.

Adaptation is at the heart of this harmonious future. As AI technologies evolve, so too must our skills and mindsets. Embracing lifelong learning and flexibility, we prepare ourselves to navigate the dynamic landscape of AI advancements. This adaptability not only enhances our ability to work alongside AI but also empowers us to harness its full potential in innovative ways.

Resonance, the fourth component, involves aligning AI developments with societal goals and values. This alignment ensures that AI serves the greater good, addressing critical global challenges such as climate change, inequality, and health crises. By resonating with the needs of society, AI becomes a catalyst for positive change, driving progress that benefits all.

Finally, Transformation is the culmination of these efforts. It is the realization of a future where AI and humans thrive together, each enhancing the other's capabilities. This transformation is not merely technological but cultural, redefining our understanding of work, creativity, and community. As we embrace this new paradigm, we unlock the potential for a renaissance of human achievement, where technology amplifies rather than diminishes our human experience.

In this envisioned future, AI and humans are not adversaries but allies, working in concert to tackle the challenges of tomorrow. By fostering a mindset of collaboration and mutual respect, we lay the groundwork for a world where technology and humanity are inextricably linked, driving progress that is both meaningful and sustainable. This harmonious future is within our grasp, requiring only our commitment to shaping it with intention and care.

Chapter 11: Technological Coexistence

Integrative Technologies

In a world increasingly defined by technological advancements, the integration of AI into the fabric of daily life represents a pivotal moment in human history. The fusion of AI and human capabilities is not merely a technological evolution but a profound transformation that challenges us to rethink the nature of work, creativity, and interaction. As we delve deeper into the concept of integrative technologies, it becomes clear that this is not just about machines learning to mimic human tasks but about creating a harmonious ecosystem where AI amplifies human potential.

The potential of integrative technologies lies in their ability to enhance human capabilities rather than replace them. This symbiosis can be seen across various domains, from healthcare to education, where AI assists professionals in making more informed decisions, thus improving outcomes. For instance, in the medical field, AI-driven diagnostic tools are not designed to replace doctors but to provide them with enhanced data analysis capabilities, leading to more accurate diagnoses and personalized treatments. Similarly, in education, AI can tailor learning experiences to individual needs, fostering a more inclusive and effective educational environment.

Integrative technologies also redefine creativity and innovation. By automating routine tasks, AI frees up human minds to focus on more complex and creative endeavors. This shift enables individuals and organizations to explore new ideas and solutions that were previously unimaginable. The creative industries, such as music, art, and design, are witnessing a renaissance, where AI acts as a collaborator rather than a competitor, generating novel forms of expression and pushing the boundaries of what is possible.

However, the journey towards integrative technologies is not without its challenges. Ethical considerations must be at the forefront of this integration, ensuring that AI is developed and deployed in ways that respect human values and rights. This requires a robust framework for evaluating the impact of AI on society, addressing concerns such as privacy, bias, and accountability. By fostering a culture of transparency and responsibility, we can mitigate potential risks and ensure that AI serves the greater good.

The HEART framework—Humanize, Evaluate, Adapt, Resonate, Transform—provides a guiding principle for navigating these challenges. It emphasizes the importance of human-centric AI development, where technology is designed to complement and enhance human abilities. By continuously evaluating and adapting to the evolving technological landscape, individuals and organizations can remain resilient and innovative in the face of change.

Ultimately, the integration of AI and human capabilities represents a new frontier in human progress. It challenges us to redefine our relationship with technology and to embrace a future where AI is not seen as a threat but as a partner in our collective journey towards a more advanced and equitable society. As we stand on the brink of this new era, it is crucial to approach integrative technologies with an open mind and a commitment to harnessing their potential for the benefit of all humanity.

Coexistence Models

In the evolving landscape of technology, the integration of artificial intelligence into human society creates a tapestry of coexistence models that redefine our interactions and future possibilities. These models are not mere theoretical constructs; they are the frameworks through which we envision a harmonious synergy between human intellect and machine precision. By examining these coexistence models, we gain insights into fostering a collaborative environment where AI becomes an extension of human capability rather than a replacement.

One of the foundational models is the augmentation paradigm, where AI tools enhance human decision-making and creativity. This model emphasizes the role of AI as an enabler, providing humans with unprecedented access to data and analytical capabilities. In this context, AI acts as an assistant, offering insights that inform and elevate human judgment. For instance, in medical diagnostics, AI systems can analyze vast datasets to identify patterns that may elude human practitioners, thereby augmenting their ability to diagnose and treat diseases effectively.

Another significant model is the symbiotic partnership, where humans and AI systems collaborate seamlessly. This model draws inspiration from biological ecosystems, where diverse species coexist and thrive through mutual benefit. In a corporate setting, this could manifest as AI-driven platforms that manage routine tasks, allowing human workers to focus on strategic and creative endeavors. The symbiosis is achieved through a shared understanding of goals and the delegation of tasks to the entity best suited to perform them, be it human or machine.

The autonomy model presents a different approach, where AI systems operate independently within set boundaries to achieve specific objectives. This model raises important ethical and operational questions about trust and accountability. Autonomous vehicles, for example, must navigate complex urban environments while ensuring passenger safety and adhering to traffic regulations. Here, the challenge lies in designing AI systems that can make autonomous decisions while remaining aligned with human values and societal norms.

In contrast, the integration model focuses on the seamless incorporation of AI into human environments, blurring the lines between human and machine capabilities. This model envisions a future where AI is embedded in all aspects of life, from smart homes that adapt to our preferences to personalized learning environments that cater to individual educational needs. The integration model challenges us to rethink the boundaries of human-machine interaction and explore new frontiers of collaboration.

These coexistence models compel us to consider the ethical implications and societal impacts of AI adoption. They highlight the necessity of a framework that prioritizes human dignity and agency while embracing technological advancement. As we navigate these models, the ultimate goal is to cultivate an ecosystem where AI and humans coexist in a manner that enhances human potential and fosters a more equitable and innovative society. In doing so, we lay the groundwork for a future where AI is not just a tool but a trusted partner in the human journey towards progress.

Human-Centric Design

In the evolving landscape of artificial intelligence, embracing a human-centric approach is paramount. This philosophy centers on the belief that technology should serve humanity, enhancing our capabilities while respecting our intrinsic values and ethics. Human-centric design is not merely about user-friendly interfaces; it is about embedding empathy and understanding into the very fabric of AI systems. This approach ensures that AI technologies are developed with a deep appreciation for human needs, aspirations, and limitations.

At its core, human-centric design requires a shift in perspective. It calls for a paradigm where human experiences and emotions are at the forefront of technological advancements. This involves an iterative process of designing, testing, and refining AI systems to align with human values and societal norms. By prioritizing human welfare and ethical considerations, we can create AI that not only complements but also elevates human potential.

Incorporating human-centric principles into AI development begins with understanding the diverse contexts in which these technologies operate. This means recognizing the cultural, social, and economic factors that influence how AI is perceived and utilized. By fostering inclusivity and diversity in AI design, we can ensure that these systems are accessible and beneficial to all segments of society, thereby reducing disparities and promoting equity.

Moreover, human-centric design emphasizes transparency and accountability. As AI systems become more complex and autonomous, it is crucial to maintain clarity about how decisions are made and who is responsible for them. This transparency builds trust between humans and machines, facilitating smoother integration of AI into everyday life. By establishing clear guidelines and ethical standards, we can mitigate potential risks and ensure that AI acts in the best interest of humanity.

The journey towards human-centric AI also involves empowering individuals with the knowledge and skills to engage with these technologies meaningfully. Education plays a pivotal role in this empowerment, equipping people with the tools to understand and influence the AI systems they interact with. By promoting digital literacy and critical thinking, we can foster a society that is not only aware of AI's capabilities but also its limitations.

Ultimately, human-centric design is about creating a harmonious relationship between humans and AI. It is a commitment to developing technologies that enhance our quality of life while preserving our fundamental rights and freedoms. By adopting this approach, we can ensure that AI serves as a catalyst for positive change, driving innovation in a manner that respects and uplifts the human spirit. This vision of AI as a partner, rather than a tool, reflects a future where technology and humanity coexist and thrive together, building a world that is more just, equitable, and compassionate.

Future Coexistence

Reflecting on the potential future of AI and human coexistence invites us to consider a landscape where technology and humanity operate in harmonious tandem. This vision is not merely a speculative dream but a plausible reality underpinned by the HEART framework principles. As we navigate this future, the synergy between human creativity and artificial intelligence becomes a cornerstone in shaping a world that honors both progress and ethical responsibility.

In this envisioned future, AI acts as an augmentation of human potential rather than a competitor. By humanizing AI, we can ensure that technological advancements are aligned with human values and societal needs. This approach requires a deliberate focus on developing AI systems that resonate with human emotions and ethical standards, creating tools that enhance rather than replace human capabilities.

The path to coexistence demands an evaluative lens through which we can assess the implications of AI in various sectors. From healthcare to education, AI offers unprecedented opportunities to optimize and innovate. However, it also presents challenges that necessitate careful consideration and strategic planning. Evaluating these risks and opportunities allows us to adapt our approaches, ensuring that AI integration is both beneficial and sustainable.

Adaptability is a critical trait in this future landscape. As AI continues to evolve, so too must our strategies for learning and development. Lifelong learning becomes a norm, empowering individuals to continuously update their skills and knowledge to keep pace with technological advancements. This adaptability fosters a dynamic interaction between humans and AI, where both entities learn from each other, driving mutual growth and understanding.

Meaningful partnerships between humans and AI are central to this coexistence. These partnerships are not transactional but transformative, characterized by a shared vision of progress that prioritizes human dignity and ethical considerations. By transforming our relationship with AI, we can unlock new avenues for creativity and innovation, positioning ourselves at the forefront of a new Renaissance of human achievement.

The future coexistence of humans and AI is predicated on a collaborative mindset that embraces AI as a partner rather than a threat. This mindset shift requires leaders, technologists, and policymakers to champion initiatives that integrate AI into the fabric of daily life while safeguarding human values and ethical principles. By doing so, we can create a future where AI and humanity thrive together, each enhancing the other in a symbiotic relationship that propels society forward.

In conclusion, the future coexistence of AI and humans offers a transformative vision of progress and harmony. By adhering to the principles of the HEART framework, we can navigate this future with confidence, ensuring that AI serves as an ally in our collective journey toward a more equitable and innovative world. This future is not just possible; it is within our reach, waiting to be realized through thoughtful collaboration and visionary leadership.

Chapter 12: AI's Impact on Society

Social Transformations

In the unfolding narrative of AI's integration into society, the transformative power it wields is both immense and multifaceted. The current epoch mirrors past societal shifts, where technology acted as a catalyst for profound change. Much like the Industrial Revolution, AI is poised to redefine the social landscape, altering how we perceive work, relationships, and the very fabric of daily life.

At the core of this transformation lies the potential for AI to augment human capabilities. By alleviating mundane tasks and enhancing decision-making processes, AI opens avenues for creativity and innovation previously unimaginable. This shift encourages a re-evaluation of human roles, pushing society towards more meaningful engagements and pursuits. The symbiotic relationship between humans and AI fosters a new form of collaboration, one where the strengths of both entities are harnessed to achieve outcomes greater than the sum of their parts.

However, this transformation is not without its challenges. As AI begins to permeate various aspects of life, questions surrounding ethics, privacy, and equity become increasingly pertinent. Ensuring that AI development and deployment are aligned with human values is crucial in navigating these social changes responsibly. The HEART framework—Humanize, Evaluate, Adapt, Resonate, Transform—offers a structured approach to addressing these issues. By prioritizing human-centric design and ethical considerations, it becomes possible to guide AI integration in ways that are beneficial and just.

The social transformations driven by AI also demand a cultural shift towards lifelong learning and adaptability. As AI continuously evolves, so too must the skills and knowledge of the workforce. This necessitates an educational paradigm that is flexible, inclusive, and forward-thinking. By fostering environments where learning is continuous and accessible, societies can better prepare for the dynamic nature of AI-driven change.

Moreover, AI's role in social transformation extends to the enhancement of community and connectivity. Digital platforms powered by AI enable unprecedented levels of interaction and collaboration across geographical boundaries. This connectivity can lead to greater cultural exchange and understanding, promoting a more cohesive global society. Yet, it also requires vigilance to ensure that digital divides do not exacerbate existing inequalities.

In embracing the social transformations heralded by AI, it is essential to maintain a balance between technological advancement and human welfare. The path forward involves not only leveraging AI's capabilities but also safeguarding the values that define humanity. By doing so, AI can become a powerful ally in crafting a future that is equitable, innovative, and inclusive. The journey of social transformation is ongoing, and its success hinges on our collective ability to navigate the complexities of this new era with wisdom and foresight.

Community Engagement

In an era where artificial intelligence is becoming increasingly integrated into the fabric of society, fostering a sense of community engagement is paramount. The Synergy Mindset emphasizes the importance of building alliances between AI technologies and human communities to unlock potential and drive societal progress. At its core, community engagement is about creating a dialogue that bridges the technological divide, fostering inclusivity and shared understanding.

To truly harness AI's capabilities, we must first acknowledge the diverse needs and perspectives within our communities. This involves actively listening to the voices that are often marginalized in the tech discourse. By doing so, we ensure that AI developments are not only technically sound but also socially equitable. In practice, this means involving community members in the design and implementation processes of AI systems, ensuring that their insights and concerns are reflected in the outcomes.

Moreover, community engagement in the context of AI should be viewed as a continuous journey rather than a one-time event. It requires ongoing efforts to educate and inform the public about AI's potential and limitations. This educational aspect is crucial, as it empowers individuals with the knowledge to participate meaningfully in discussions about AI's role in society. Workshops, seminars, and collaborative projects can serve as platforms for such engagement, allowing for an exchange of ideas and fostering a sense of ownership over technological advancements.

Another critical aspect of community engagement is transparency. Communities must be kept informed about how AI systems are being deployed and the data that is being collected. Transparency builds trust, which is essential for the successful integration of AI into everyday life. When communities understand and trust AI technologies, they are more likely to support and adopt them, leading to more effective and beneficial outcomes.

Furthermore, engaging communities with AI requires addressing ethical considerations head-on. This means developing AI systems that are not only efficient but also fair, accountable, and aligned with societal values. By prioritizing ethics in AI development, we can mitigate risks and prevent the perpetuation of biases and inequalities. This ethical focus should be a collaborative effort involving technologists, ethicists, policymakers, and community members alike.

In summary, community engagement in the age of AI is about fostering a collaborative spirit that respects and harnesses the strengths of both technology and humanity. It is about creating systems that not only enhance human capabilities but also respect human dignity and promote social good. Through thoughtful and inclusive engagement, we can create a future where AI serves as a catalyst for positive change, enhancing the quality of life for all members of society.

Global Implications

As artificial intelligence continues to evolve, its global implications become increasingly profound, touching every corner of society. The interplay between AI and human capabilities offers unprecedented opportunities but also presents unique challenges that require careful consideration. Central to this dynamic is the need to balance innovation with ethical responsibility, ensuring that AI serves as a force for good rather than a catalyst for disparity or conflict.

The potential for AI to drive economic growth is undeniable. By automating routine tasks and enhancing decision-making processes, AI can significantly boost productivity across various sectors. This technological leap forward has the power to transform industries, from healthcare to finance, by streamlining operations and introducing new efficiencies. However, this shift also necessitates a reevaluation of workforce dynamics. As machines take on more roles traditionally held by humans, there is an urgent need for reskilling and upskilling to prepare the workforce for an AI-integrated future.

Moreover, AI's global implications extend beyond economics, influencing the geopolitical landscape. Nations that successfully harness AI could gain significant competitive advantages, potentially leading to shifts in global power balances. This reality underscores the importance of fostering international cooperation and dialogue to ensure that AI development is guided by shared principles and mutual interests, rather than unilateral pursuits that could exacerbate tensions.

In the realm of ethics, AI presents complex dilemmas that transcend borders. The potential for bias in AI systems, driven by flawed data or algorithms, highlights the need for rigorous oversight and accountability. It is crucial to develop frameworks that promote transparency and fairness, preventing AI from perpetuating or amplifying existing inequalities. This ethical stewardship is not just a national concern but a global imperative, requiring collaboration across cultures and disciplines to establish equitable standards.

AI's transformative potential also extends to addressing some of the world's most pressing challenges. From climate change to healthcare disparities, AI can offer innovative solutions that were previously unimaginable. For instance, AI-driven models can predict environmental changes with greater accuracy, enabling more effective interventions. In healthcare, AI can assist in diagnosing diseases and personalizing treatment plans, improving outcomes and accessibility for patients worldwide.

However, realizing these benefits requires a concerted effort to democratize AI access and benefits. Ensuring that AI advancements are inclusive and equitable is essential to prevent a digital divide where only a few reap the rewards. This involves investing in education and infrastructure, particularly in underrepresented regions, to empower all communities to participate in and benefit from AI developments.

Ultimately, the global implications of AI hinge on our collective ability to navigate its complexities thoughtfully and inclusively. By fostering a mindset that embraces collaboration, ethical responsibility, and shared progress, we can harness AI's potential to enhance human capabilities and address global challenges. This requires visionary leadership and a commitment to building a future where AI is not just a tool, but a partner in creating a more equitable and prosperous world.

Future Society

In contemplating the future society, a profound transformation emerges as humanity and artificial intelligence coalesce in a symbiotic relationship. This unfolding narrative is not merely a tale of technological advancement but a reimagining of human potential in the digital age. The confluence of AI and human ingenuity heralds a new era where technology enhances rather than diminishes our human experience.

As AI continues to integrate into the fabric of daily life, it reshapes societal structures, creating opportunities for enriched human interaction and collaboration. In this future society, AI acts as a catalyst for innovation, empowering individuals to transcend traditional limitations and explore new dimensions of creativity and problem-solving. The synergy between AI and humans fosters environments where ideas flourish, and diverse perspectives converge to address complex challenges.

Central to this transformation is the HEART framework, a guiding principle that emphasizes Humanize, Evaluate, Adapt, Resonate, and Transform. This framework serves as a compass for navigating the ethical and practical dimensions of AI integration. By humanizing technology, we ensure that AI remains aligned with human values, promoting empathy and understanding in its applications.

Evaluating the impact of AI on various facets of society, from healthcare to education, is paramount. It involves a continuous assessment of both risks and opportunities, ensuring that AI's deployment is both responsible and beneficial. Adapting to the rapid technological evolution requires a commitment to lifelong learning, equipping individuals with the skills needed to thrive in an AI-enhanced world.

Resonating with AI involves creating systems that are not only efficient but also resonate with human emotions and cultural nuances. This resonance fosters a deeper connection between humans and technology, ensuring that AI solutions are not only technically sound but also socially relevant.

The transformative potential of AI lies in its ability to drive progress without dehumanization. In this future society, AI is a partner in the human journey, enhancing our capabilities while preserving the essence of what it means to be human. This partnership facilitates the emergence of a new Renaissance, where human creativity and AI innovation converge to unlock unprecedented possibilities.

The vision of a future society where AI and humans coexist harmoniously is not without its challenges. It demands vigilant stewardship to navigate ethical dilemmas and ensure equitable access to technological advancements. Policymakers, technologists, and leaders must collaborate to shape policies that promote inclusivity and prevent the exacerbation of existing inequalities.

As we stand on the cusp of this future, the narrative of AI and human collaboration is still being written. It is a story of potential and promise, where the choices made today will define the contours of tomorrow's society. Embracing this future requires courage, creativity, and a steadfast commitment to a vision where technology serves humanity, enriching our lives and expanding the horizons of what is possible.

Chapter 13: Shaping the AI Future

Visionary Leadership

Visionary leadership in the context of AI and human collaboration is about transcending conventional boundaries and embracing a future where technology and humanity evolve together. This leadership style requires a profound understanding of both the opportunities and challenges posed by artificial intelligence. It demands a mindset that looks beyond the immediate gains and envisions a long-term symbiosis between human creativity and technological prowess.

At the heart of visionary leadership is the ability to perceive AI not as a mere tool but as a partner in innovation. This perspective shifts the narrative from one of competition to collaboration, where AI augments human capabilities rather than replacing them. Leaders with this vision recognize that the true potential of AI lies in its ability to complement human intelligence, driving unprecedented advancements across various fields.

A crucial aspect of visionary leadership is ethical foresight. As AI continues to permeate every aspect of life, leaders must navigate the ethical landscape with caution and responsibility. This involves setting a moral compass that guides AI development and deployment, ensuring that these technologies are used to enhance human well-being and societal progress. Ethical leadership in the AI era is about balancing innovation with integrity, fostering trust in AI systems, and advocating for policies that protect human rights and dignity.

Visionary leaders are also characterized by their adaptability. In a rapidly changing technological environment, the ability to pivot and innovate is essential. These leaders are lifelong learners who remain open to new ideas and perspectives, constantly seeking to understand the evolving nature of AI and its implications. They encourage a culture of continuous improvement and resilience, preparing their organizations and societies to thrive amidst change.

Furthermore, visionary leadership in AI involves cultivating a collaborative ecosystem. This means building networks and alliances that transcend traditional industry silos, bringing together diverse stakeholders to co-create solutions. By fostering interdisciplinary collaboration, leaders can harness the collective intelligence of varied fields, leading to more holistic and impactful AI applications.

Inspiring a shared vision is another hallmark of visionary leadership. Effective leaders communicate a compelling narrative about the future of AI and humanity, one that resonates with and mobilizes people towards common goals. They articulate the benefits of AI-human synergy in a way that is accessible and engaging, helping individuals and organizations see their role in this transformative journey.

Ultimately, visionary leadership is about crafting a future where AI and humans coexist harmoniously, leveraging the strengths of each to address global challenges and create a better world. It is about guiding humanity through the complexities of the AI revolution with wisdom, courage, and compassion, ensuring that this new era is marked by progress and prosperity for all.

Policy Development

In the ever-evolving landscape of artificial intelligence, the development of policies that guide its integration with human endeavors is crucial. This subchapter delves into the intricacies of policy development, emphasizing the need for a balanced approach that aligns technological advancement with human-centric values. The HEART framework serves as a foundational guide, advocating for policies that prioritize humanization, ethical evaluation, adaptability, resonance, and transformative potential.

The journey begins with recognizing the dual nature of AI as both a tool and a partner. Policies should not merely regulate AI but also harness its capabilities to enhance human creativity and innovation. This requires a shift in perspective, viewing AI as an ally that can augment human potential rather than as a competitor. By fostering a collaborative mindset, policies can pave the way for AI to be integrated seamlessly into various sectors, from healthcare to education.

Ethical evaluation stands at the forefront of policy development. It is imperative that policies are designed to safeguard against potential risks while maximizing benefits. This involves a continuous process of assessing the implications of AI applications, ensuring they align with societal values and ethical standards. Policymakers must engage with diverse stakeholders, including technologists, ethicists, and the public, to create a comprehensive ethical framework that guides AI integration.

Adaptability is another cornerstone of effective policy development. In a rapidly advancing technological landscape, policies must be dynamic, capable of evolving in response to new developments. This requires a proactive approach, anticipating future challenges and opportunities, and preparing to adapt policies accordingly. By fostering a culture of lifelong learning and adaptability, policies can ensure that both individuals and institutions remain agile in the face of change.

The concept of resonance emphasizes the importance of policies that resonate with the broader societal goals of inclusivity and equity. AI policies should aim to bridge gaps, ensuring that the benefits of AI are accessible to all, regardless of socio-economic status. This involves addressing issues of digital divide and ensuring that AI technologies are designed and implemented with an inclusive mindset.

Transformative potential is the ultimate goal of AI policy development. Policies should be crafted to not only regulate and guide but also to inspire transformative change. By envisioning a future where AI and humans work in harmony, policies can drive progress towards a more sustainable and equitable world. This requires a visionary approach, one that looks beyond immediate concerns to consider the long-term impact of AI on society.

In crafting policies for AI, it is essential to maintain a balance between innovation and regulation. Policies should encourage experimentation and creativity while ensuring that such pursuits are grounded in ethical considerations. By drawing on historical parallels, such as the Industrial Revolution, policymakers can learn from past experiences to navigate the complexities of AI integration effectively.

Ultimately, the development of AI policies is an ongoing process, one that requires collaboration, foresight, and a commitment to human-centric values. By embracing the principles of the HEART framework, policymakers can guide the integration of AI in a manner that amplifies human potential and fosters a future where technology and humanity coexist in harmony.

Strategic Frameworks

In the ever-evolving landscape of technology and human interaction, strategic frameworks play a pivotal role in harmonizing AI with human endeavors. The integration of AI into various sectors demands a thoughtful approach that transcends mere functionality, aiming instead for a symbiotic relationship that enhances both human and machine capabilities. This chapter delves into the strategic frameworks essential for achieving such synergy, focusing on principles that ensure AI acts as a complement to human intelligence rather than a replacement.

Central to this discussion is the HEART framework, which serves as a guiding philosophy for integrating AI responsibly and effectively. This framework emphasizes the importance of humanizing technology by ensuring that AI systems are designed with empathy and understanding at their core. By prioritizing human values and ethical considerations, organizations can create AI solutions that resonate with users and foster trust.

Evaluating AI systems critically is another cornerstone of strategic frameworks. This involves a thorough assessment of the risks and opportunities associated with AI deployment in various industries. From healthcare to finance, each sector presents unique challenges that require tailored strategies to navigate. By adopting a proactive approach to evaluation, stakeholders can anticipate potential pitfalls and leverage AI's strengths to drive innovation and efficiency.

Adaptation is crucial in the dynamic world of AI. As technologies evolve at an unprecedented pace, organizations must cultivate a culture of continuous learning and flexibility. This mindset enables them to stay ahead of the curve and adapt to new developments swiftly. By embracing change and fostering an environment of lifelong learning, businesses and individuals can harness AI's potential to transform their operations and achieve sustainable growth.

Resonating with stakeholders is another vital aspect of strategic frameworks. Successful AI integration involves engaging all relevant parties, from employees to customers, in the development process. By involving diverse perspectives, organizations can ensure that AI solutions are inclusive and address the needs of all users. This collaborative approach not only enhances the effectiveness of AI systems but also strengthens the relationship between technology and its beneficiaries.

Finally, the transformation element of the HEART framework underscores the transformative potential of AI when strategically integrated. By leveraging AI's capabilities, organizations can drive meaningful change across various domains, from streamlining processes to unlocking new avenues for creativity and innovation. This transformative impact extends beyond the organizational level, influencing societal progress and shaping a future where AI and humans coexist harmoniously.

In summary, strategic frameworks provide the blueprint for navigating the complexities of AI integration. By focusing on human-centric values, critical evaluation, adaptability, stakeholder engagement, and transformative potential, these frameworks empower organizations to harness AI responsibly and effectively. As we move forward into an AI-driven era, these principles will serve as the foundation for a future where technology enhances human potential and contributes to a more equitable and prosperous world.

Future Directions

As we look to the horizon, the integration of AI into the human experience presents both opportunities and challenges that demand thoughtful navigation. The future of AI-human collaboration hinges on our ability to foster an environment where technology enhances human capabilities rather than replacing them. This requires a paradigm shift in how we perceive and interact with AI, moving from a tool-centric perspective to one that embraces AI as a collaborative partner in innovation and creativity.

Central to this future is the HEART framework, which guides this transition by emphasizing the importance of humanizing technology. This involves developing AI systems that are not only efficient but also ethically aligned with human values. By prioritizing empathy and ethical considerations, we can ensure that AI development remains grounded in principles that respect human dignity and promote societal well-being.

Evaluation of AI's role in various sectors will be crucial as we advance. Industries such as healthcare, finance, and education stand to benefit immensely from AI-driven insights and automation. However, with these advancements come risks that must be carefully managed. By adopting a proactive approach to risk assessment and mitigation, we can harness AI's potential while safeguarding against unintended consequences.

Adaptability will be a defining trait of successful AI-human partnerships. As AI technologies evolve, so too must our approaches to integrating them into existing systems. This requires a commitment to lifelong learning and continuous skill development, ensuring that individuals and organizations remain agile in the face of rapid technological change.

Resonance between AI and human creativity will unlock new avenues for innovation. By leveraging AI's computational power, we can enhance human artistic and intellectual pursuits, leading to breakthroughs that were previously unimaginable. This symbiotic relationship will redefine the boundaries of what is possible, ushering in a new era of creative exploration.

Transformation is the ultimate goal of AI-human collaboration. By aligning AI development with transformative societal goals, we can address some of the world's most pressing challenges, from climate change to global inequality. This requires a concerted effort to align technological advancements with sustainable development objectives, ensuring that progress is inclusive and equitable.

The path forward is one of cautious optimism. By embracing a mindset that values collaboration, ethical responsibility, and continuous adaptation, we can shape a future where AI serves as a catalyst for human flourishing. This vision requires the collective efforts of leaders, technologists, and policymakers to create frameworks that support responsible AI integration and foster a culture of innovation that respects human values.

In navigating this future, we must remain vigilant in our commitment to ethical AI development, ensuring that technology serves humanity's best interests. By doing so, we can create a world where AI and humans coexist harmoniously, each enhancing the other's potential and paving the way for a brighter, more equitable future.

Chapter 14: Embracing the AI Journey

Personal Growth

In a world where artificial intelligence is rapidly evolving, the essence of personal growth lies in our ability to synergize with these technological advancements. The journey of self-improvement is no longer a solitary path but a collaborative dance with AI, a tool that can amplify our innate potential. As we navigate this new landscape, the HEART framework offers a beacon, guiding us to humanize our interactions with AI, ensuring that our growth remains anchored in humanity.

The first step in this transformative process is understanding that AI is not a competitor but a collaborator in our personal development. By embracing AI as a partner, we can unlock new opportunities for learning and creativity, allowing us to expand our horizons beyond traditional boundaries. This partnership encourages us to evaluate our strengths and weaknesses with a fresh perspective, leveraging AI's analytical prowess to gain insights that were previously inaccessible.

Adaptability becomes crucial as we integrate AI into our personal growth strategies. The rapid pace of technological change requires us to cultivate a mindset of continuous learning, where we are open to evolving alongside these innovations. This adaptability not only enhances our ability to thrive in an AI-driven world but also empowers us to harness AI's capabilities to drive our personal and professional goals forward.

Resonance with AI is achieved when we align our values and aspirations with the potential that AI offers. This alignment ensures that our growth is not just technical but also ethical, as we strive to create meaningful connections that resonate with our deeper purpose. By fostering this resonance, we cultivate a sense of fulfillment that transcends mere achievement, enriching our lives with purpose and direction.

Transformation, the ultimate goal of personal growth, is realized when we integrate AI into our daily lives in a way that enhances our humanity rather than diminishing it. This transformation is not about becoming more like machines but about using machines to become more human. It is about leveraging AI to elevate our empathy, creativity, and ethical decision-making, ensuring that our growth is holistic and inclusive.

By viewing AI as an ally in our personal growth journey, we open ourselves to a future where technology and humanity coexist in harmony. This harmonious relationship is the cornerstone of the synergy mindset, a paradigm that empowers us to embrace AI's potential while remaining true to our core values. As we continue to evolve, this mindset will guide us in shaping a future where personal growth is not just possible but limitless, fueled by the synergy of human and artificial intelligence.

Collective Progress

In the unfolding narrative of human development, the collaboration between artificial intelligence and human intellect stands as a monumental chapter. This synergy is not merely a convergence of technology and humanity; it is a profound transformation of how progress is defined and achieved. As we navigate the complexities of this new era, the collective advancement of societies hinges on our ability to integrate AI into the very fabric of human endeavor.

The historical context offers us valuable insights into how collective progress has been achieved in the past. The printing press, for instance, revolutionized the dissemination of knowledge, democratizing information and sparking an unprecedented era of enlightenment. Similarly, the Industrial Revolution redefined production and labor, paving the way for modern economies. Today, AI holds the potential to surpass these milestones, offering tools that can enhance human capabilities in unimaginable ways. However, the key lies in ensuring that this progress is inclusive and equitable.

Collective progress in the age of AI requires a reevaluation of our traditional systems of education and workforce development. It is imperative that education systems evolve to foster skills that complement AI technologies. Critical thinking, creativity, and emotional intelligence must be at the forefront of curricula, ensuring that future generations are equipped not only to work alongside AI but to innovate with it. In the workplace, AI should be seen as a collaborator rather than a competitor, augmenting human tasks and freeing individuals to engage in more meaningful and creative work.

Moreover, the ethical considerations surrounding AI cannot be overlooked. As AI systems become more integrated into societal functions, the responsibility of guiding these systems with ethical frameworks becomes paramount. Collective progress is rooted in the shared values of humanity, and it is these values that must guide the development and deployment of AI technologies. By fostering a culture of transparency and accountability, we can ensure that AI serves the common good, enhancing rather than detracting from human dignity.

The potential for AI to contribute to collective progress is vast, yet it requires a concerted effort from all sectors of society. Policymakers, technologists, educators, and citizens must collaborate to create environments where AI can thrive as a partner in human progress. This collaboration should aim to address the disparities that technology can exacerbate, ensuring that the benefits of AI are distributed fairly across all communities.

As we look to the future, the concept of collective progress in the age of AI is not just about technological advancement. It is about reimagining what it means to progress as a society, where technology amplifies human potential and fosters a deeper connection among individuals and communities. This vision of progress is one where AI and humanity move forward together, crafting a future that is as much about human values as it is about technological prowess. The journey towards this future is paved with challenges and opportunities, but with a shared commitment to synergy, the possibilities are boundless.

Continuous Exploration

Continuous exploration in the realm of AI and human collaboration revolves around the perpetual quest for knowledge and understanding. This pursuit is not merely about seeking new technologies or algorithms but about cultivating a mindset that is open to the evolving landscape of artificial intelligence. In this context, exploration becomes a dynamic process, one that requires constant adaptation and reflection to fully harness the potential of AI.

Within this framework, the role of curiosity cannot be overstated. It is the driving force that propels both individuals and organizations to push beyond the boundaries of current understanding. By fostering an environment where questioning and inquiry are encouraged, we enable the discovery of novel insights and solutions that can redefine our relationship with technology.

Moreover, continuous exploration necessitates a willingness to embrace uncertainty. The future of AI is inherently unpredictable, with advancements occurring at a rapid pace. To thrive in such an environment, one must be comfortable with ambiguity and possess the flexibility to pivot strategies as new information emerges. This adaptability is crucial for staying ahead in a world where the only constant is change.

In practice, this means engaging with AI not as a static tool, but as a dynamic partner. It involves iterative experimentation, where hypotheses are tested, refined, and retested in a cycle of ongoing learning. This approach mirrors the scientific method, where each experiment builds upon the last, contributing to a deeper understanding of the capabilities and limitations of AI.

Furthermore, continuous exploration is a collaborative endeavor. It requires the integration of diverse perspectives and expertise to fully grasp the multifaceted nature of AI. By bringing together stakeholders from different fields, we can ensure that the development of AI is aligned with broader societal values and goals. This interdisciplinary collaboration is essential for creating AI systems that are not only innovative but also ethical and inclusive.

At its core, continuous exploration is about cultivating a culture of lifelong learning. In a world where AI is increasingly becoming a part of everyday life, staying informed and educated about its developments is paramount. This means investing in education and training programs that equip individuals with the skills needed to navigate an AI-driven future. It also involves creating pathways for ongoing professional development, ensuring that the workforce remains agile and prepared for the challenges and opportunities that lie ahead.

Ultimately, continuous exploration is a journey without a destination. It is about embracing the unknown and viewing each new discovery as a stepping stone towards greater understanding. By maintaining an open and inquisitive mindset, we can unlock the full potential of AI, transforming it from a tool of automation into a catalyst for human progress. In doing so, we pave the way for a future where AI and humanity coexist in harmony, each enhancing the capabilities of the other.

Enduring Synergy

In the vast tapestry of human advancement, the relationship between artificial intelligence and human endeavor is a dynamic interplay that promises to redefine our future. This synergy is not merely a convergence of technology and humanity but a sustained partnership that can lead to unprecedented progress. As we delve into this transformative journey, it's essential to understand how AI and human intelligence can coalesce to forge a path that is both innovative and ethically grounded.

The potential for enduring synergy lies in our ability to harness AI's capabilities while preserving and enhancing human values. This requires a nuanced approach that respects the complexity of both entities. By fostering an environment where AI is seen as a collaborator rather than a competitor, we can unlock new realms of creativity and problem-solving. The HEART framework serves as a guide in this endeavor, emphasizing the need to Humanize our interactions with AI, Evaluate its impacts critically, Adapt to its evolving nature, Resonate with our core values, and Transform our societal structures accordingly.

A critical aspect of this enduring relationship is the recognition of AI's role in augmenting human potential. Rather than viewing AI as a replacement for human labor, we should see it as a tool that enhances our capabilities. In fields ranging from healthcare to education, AI has the potential to revolutionize the way we approach complex challenges, providing insights and efficiencies that were previously unimaginable. However, this requires a shift in mindset, where continuous learning and adaptation become integral to our professional lives.

Moreover, the ethical considerations surrounding AI must be at the forefront of our efforts to integrate it into society. As AI systems become more sophisticated, the responsibility to ensure they align with human values becomes paramount. This involves not only the developers and engineers who create these systems but also policymakers, educators, and the public at large. By fostering a culture of transparency and accountability, we can build trust in AI technologies and ensure they serve the greater good.

The enduring synergy between AI and humans also hinges on our ability to innovate responsibly. As we push the boundaries of what AI can achieve, we must remain vigilant about its potential risks. This includes addressing issues such as data privacy, algorithmic bias, and the displacement of jobs. By proactively tackling these challenges, we can mitigate potential downsides and ensure that the benefits of AI are widely distributed.

Ultimately, the future of AI and human collaboration is one that holds immense promise. It is a future where technology empowers us to reach new heights, where creativity and innovation are boundless, and where societal progress is driven by a harmonious blend of human and artificial intelligence. By embracing this vision, we can create a world that is not only technologically advanced but also deeply rooted in the principles of equity, justice, and human dignity. In this landscape, the enduring synergy between AI and humans is not just a possibility—it is an imperative for the continued evolution of our species.

www.ingramcontent.com/pod-product-compliance
Lightning Source LLC
LaVergne TN
LVHW022124060326
832903LV00063B/3633